Exploring Character Through Structural Metaphor

Exploring Character Through Structural Metaphor will help performers discover new and valuable insights into the characters they play.

Grounded in a contemporary approach to understanding and applying the power of metaphor, it offers a practical guide for both actors and directors. This book introduces the idea of metaphor as a way of thinking rather than simply as clever comparison or figurative language. It demonstrates limitations of ways metaphor has traditionally been used in character development and presents a method for applying structural metaphor to discover rich, in-depth character insights. For directors, the model can serve as an option for guiding character analysis that is less individualistic and actor-specific and more wholistic and cast-inclusive, promoting stronger overall performance unity and production cohesion. In addition to offering a clear, followable guide for character analysis, the authors draw on personal experience to vividly demonstrate how applying this method for character analysis could impact performance and production.

This book will be a useful addition to an actor's or director's set of character development resources.

John Gribas is Professor and Associate Dean for Fine Arts and Humanities at Idaho State University, USA.

Angeline Underwood has decades of experience as an actor and director. She earned both an MA in Theatre and an MA in Communication from Idaho State University, USA.

Routledge Advances in Theatre & Performance Studies

This series is our home for cutting-edge, upper-level scholarly studies and edited collections. Considering theatre and performance alongside topics such as religion, politics, gender, race, ecology, and the avant-garde, titles are characterized by dynamic interventions into established subjects and innovative studies on emerging topics.

Screened Stages
On Theatre in Film
Rachel Joseph

Of Kings and Clowns
Leadership in Contemporary Egyptian Theatre Since 1967
Tiran Manucharyan

Female Playwrights and Applied Intersectionality in Romanian Theater
Cătălina Florina Florescu

Exploring Character Through Structural Metaphor
A Guide for Actors and Directors
John Gribas and Angeline Underwood

For more information about this series, please visit: www.routledge.com/Routledge-Advances-in-Theatre—Performance-Studies/book-series/RATPS

Exploring Character Through Structural Metaphor

A Guide for Actors and Directors

John Gribas and Angeline Underwood

LONDON AND NEW YORK

First published 2024
by Routledge
4 Park Square, Milton Park, Abingdon, Oxon OX14 4RN

and by Routledge
605 Third Avenue, New York, NY 10158

Routledge is an imprint of the Taylor & Francis Group, an informa business

British Library Cataloguing-in-Publication Data
A catalogue record for this book is available from the British Library

ISBN: 9781032376059 (hbk)
ISBN: 9781032376066 (pbk)
ISBN: 9781003341024 (ebk)

DOI: 10.4324/9781003341024

Typeset in Times New Roman
by Newgen Publishing UK

Contents

Section I

About metaphors

1 How we usually understand metaphor

In this book, we will be proposing a new model to guide character analysis. Our hope is that this model will be a helpful tool for both actors and directors. We want to be clear from the outset that we are in no way trying to replace the teaching and application of well-known, well-loved, and established methods for character analysis. Instead, we intend to offer one more tool you can add to your character analysis tool belt. Of course, we do think this new model offers something unique; otherwise, it really wouldn't make much sense for us to take the time to explain it to you or for you to read, consider, and hopefully put into practice these ideas. One advantage we see in our model is that it can be applied by actors in their own personal character exploration, but it can also be used by directors to guide not just individual actors but entire casts. In this way, it can offer a unifying dramatic framework for the complete action of a play.

We will explain this and more about the potential and payoffs of what we are proposing for character analysis later in the book. But before we can do that, we need to begin by noting that our model is grounded in the idea of metaphor. More specifically, it is grounded in a particular understanding of a particular kind of metaphor—what we will be calling "structural" metaphor. If you happen to be a cognitive linguist, you might feel completely comfortable just accepting that statement and moving along to the application. For most of us, the general idea of metaphor may feel like a very familiar thing, but we probably are a bit less confident that we fully grasp the particulars and nuances of this notion of structural metaphor—a notion that extends

DOI: 10.4324/9781003341024-2

from the broader understanding that metaphor is less a creative way of expressing a specific idea and more the fundamental way of understanding virtually everything. If that doesn't sound like metaphor as you know it, don't worry. We will fully explain the idea of structural metaphor and then show how it can be applied to character analysis. To help in that, though, let's first take some time to reflect on ways metaphor can be and typically has been understood.

Metaphor as a figure of speech

The understanding of metaphor as a figure of speech, as a sort of cosmetic or ornamental form of language used to embellish an idea, is both widespread and long-lived. In their book exploring how modern media has used metaphor to frame war, Steuter and Wills (2009) point out that this idea of metaphor as ornamental language can be traced back to the days of ancient Greece and Rome. In these classical cultures and periods, the use of metaphor was broadly considered to be "a decorative addition to literal language" and was regarded as a "fancy expression" and a way to dress up ideas, making them more interesting and palatable to an audience by "raising diction to a level beyond the commonplace and familiar" (p. 5).

An ornament is something we look at, and so to say that metaphor is "ornamental" is to suggest it is largely a visual thing. Similarly, a "figure" suggests something recognized by sight, and so defining metaphor as a figure of speech also emphasizes its visual nature. Given this, it is not surprising that metaphor is commonly seen as the use of words to create a mental picture of some idea by expressing it in a creative and visual way. As a way to reinforce how closely tied metaphor is to the visual experience, we can look to the ideas and words of Michael Lydon. Lydon is a performer and musician who writes about these artistic forms, as well as on the process of writing itself. In an online posting titled "The Power of Metaphor," Lydon argues that "metaphor acts as writing's parallax, the two-sided vision of our eyes which, when resolved by the brain, creates our picture of the spacious world" (2010, para. 10). Lydon's reference to "vision" and "eyes" and "picture" here offers a good illustration of just how strong the connection between the visual and the metaphorical is understood to be.

Most people will have no difficulty with this idea that, fundamentally, metaphor is a way to dress up otherwise plain language. At the same time, Michael Lydon's thoughtful observations on the power of metaphor suggest that there may be something more to metaphor than simply a kind of ornamental impact. In fact, there are ways to see metaphor as more than mere fanciful language, while still understanding it as a figure of speech.

Some would agree that metaphor is a figure of speech but would also argue that, as such, metaphor can be seen to highlight particular characteristics of one thing in order to better understand another. This reflection of the characteristics of one thing onto another is called linguistic transference. Perhaps this is what Lydon was suggesting when he described metaphor as "the two-sided vision of our eyes" which has impact "when resolved by the brain" and "creates our picture of the spacious world" (2010, para. 10). The Oxford English Dictionary (OED) defines metaphor as "a figure of speech in which a name or descriptive word or phrase is transferred to an object or action different from, but analogous to, that to which it is literally applicable; an instance of this, a metaphorical expression" (OED, 2015). Hopefully it is clear that an understanding of metaphor as linguistic transference goes beyond simple ornamentation. Understood this way, metaphor is a tool that can help to clarify an idea—especially a complex, confusing, or unfamiliar idea—by associating aspects of that idea with something less complex, less confusing, or more familiar.

Let us try to reinforce this distinction between ornamentation and linguistic transference. To do so, we will use…well…a metaphor!

Imagine that you own and run a small theatre company called "Palomino Playhouse" in a quaint Western resort town that is filled with shops, galleries, museums, and other businesses that cater to the constant stream of tourists passing through or stopping for a night or two. However, as the town has grown in size and tourist volume and number of businesses, you have started to see your own audience numbers diminish. With all the competition for tourists' attention, fewer and fewer are stopping in to buy tickets and enjoy a performance.

Based on some marketing data, you learn that many people simply are not aware of your theatre company. Numerous interesting shops and businesses have built up around your space over the years, and where you once clearly stood out in the city center as a great option to passers-by, you now are but one space in a sea of interesting spaces, and passers-by are largely just passing by. When you stop to think about it, the theatre building is rather plain—all one rather bland color that certainly is not eye-catching in any way. So, you decide that making your space more visually distinctive and appealing might help. You decide that brightening up the facility with a nice paint job would be a good first step. Soon, your theatre façade looks fresh and new and is far more colorful than it was. It also is more colorful than the businesses around you and clearly stands out. You hope and trust that it will grab the attention of more potential patrons.

Now imagine that, instead of settling for a new coat of paint, you decided also to invest in a large billboard located on the main road just as people are about to enter town. The billboard is not actually a part of your theatre venue. It is a very different kind of structure in a different location. But it is far more visible and directly accessible to anyone and everyone driving through than is your theatre space itself which sits on one particular street within the town and is surrounded by other businesses and visual distractions. On that billboard, though, you have the words "Palomino Playhouse" in large colorful letters—maybe the same colors as those you used to revive the façade of the theatre. You might also have other information like "one mile ahead to Center Street and two blocks to your right" or "shows the whole family will enjoy" or "half-priced matinees every Thursday through Saturday."

In this illustration, we could say that painting your theatre building is comparable to using metaphor for simple ornamentation. The paint (metaphor) makes something that is plain, simple, or easy to overlook more attention-getting. It adds emphasis. The billboard, however, is something more. It is a separate thing, but the impact comes in the relationship made in the minds of the traveling tourists—a relationship between the billboard and your theatre. And you are counting on tourists making certain kinds of connections. You want them to associate the colors used on the billboard to help them look for and identify your similarly colored theatre space. And you want them to associate with your theatre the ideas of the distance and direction to your location and the family-friendly nature of your shows and the affordability of your matinee performances. Thus, the billboard is comparable to the idea that metaphor has the power of linguistic transference. It does not simply draw attention to your theatre, but it creates a connection between billboard and theatre and, more specifically, between certain aspects of the billboard and what you want people to believe and anticipate in regard to the Palomino Playhouse.

Continuing with the idea of linguistic transference, take, for example, the metaphoric expression, "I will now shed some light on the issue." This common metaphoric phrase links a rather abstract idea, "comprehension," to the much more familiar and tangible ideas of "light" and, by extension, "dark." Valenzano and Braden (2015) consider this expression in their discussion of the use of metaphor in effective public speaking. They state, "Obviously, there is no actual light, but a lack of understanding is compared to darkness, and the speaker's intention to provide knowledge is compared to illuminating that darkness through providing light" (p. 368). Even though the ideas of "comprehension" and "light" are vastly different, the metaphor generates associations between the two ideas, and a relationship and resonance between them can be noted and used for heightened understanding. Again, looking back to the words of musician, performer, and writer, Michael Lydon, the making of a linguistic association between the ideas of "light" and "comprehension" is a "two-sided vision of our eyes which, when resolved by the brain, creates our picture of the spacious world" (2010, para. 10).

As a final example, let's look to our own William Shakespeare, metaphor master and one of the most prolific writers in history. Although more than four hundred years old, his works still connect with contemporary audiences and employ a vast and distinctive universe of metaphors. Shakespeare's use of metaphor has been the subject of much study (see Albala, 2014; Dolan, 2002; Lewis, 2012; Sullivan & Banding, 2014; Thompson & Thompson, 1987). One of Shakespeare's most recognized and repeated metaphors can be found in *As You like It*, when Jaques explains:

> All the world's a stage,
> And all the men and women merely players;
> They have their exits and their entrances
> And one man in his time plays many parts.
>
> (*As You Like It*, 2.7)

In this, Shakespeare is offering more than a clever turn of phrase; Shakespeare is clarifying and drawing attention to certain aspects of the notion of "the world" by associating it with some particular aspects of the notion of "the stage." The concept of "the world" is vast and ambiguous. Where does one start when trying to comprehend such a substantial idea? Because "the world" is so general, so indefinite, and so huge, an understanding of it can best be reached through the use of metaphor. Shakespeare uses the more defined, localized, limited concept of "stage" to help his audience grasp certain things about the more abstract concept of "the world." In addition to being more defined and limited, the idea of the "stage" is also more familiar. Shakespeare certainly could make this assumption since his words were written with the understanding that they would be heard by individuals physically sitting or standing in an actual theatre watching a performance on a physical stage, seeing actors play roles and make entrances and exits. Shakespeare's words bring "stage" and "world" into relationship and help hearers grasp the idea that, as members of the much broader "world," they play various roles in scenes in life they both enter and exit, moving from one life experience to the next.

Are metaphors figures of speech? Of course they are. They do draw attention. They also bring the unclear, intangible, and unfamiliar into relationship with the clear, tangible, and familiar in a way that draws attention to particular things to offer better understanding. This is the way metaphor has most commonly been understood.

Metaphor as a means of persuasion

As figures of speech, metaphors draw attention and bring understanding, typically using colorful and vivid language to create mental images and transferring aspects of one idea onto another. But, for many, its potential doesn't stop there. Metaphor can be seen to influence opinions, attitudes, and behavior when used as a persuasive tactic or a tool for framing. By "framing," we mean the shaping of messages by "choosing one particular meaning (or set of meanings) over another" (Fairhurst & Sarr, 1996, p. 3). Photographers influence what and how we see by making conscious, strategic decisions about what ends up inside and outside the visual frame that constitutes an image. Similarly, media professionals and advertisers make conscious, strategic decisions about what goes into and what stays out of their messages. They use metaphor to frame their persuasive appeals in an attempt to get audiences to accept their ideas and, often, to purchase their products or services. As Septianto, Pontes, and Tjiptono (2021) observe, "The use of metaphor has become an established communication tool used to enhance the persuasiveness of advertising messages" (p. 951). Indeed, the bombardment of metaphoric persuasive appeals is apparent—some would say overwhelmingly apparent—across the media in commercials, news broadcasts, and print advertisements.

Throughout history, metaphoric framing has been used by political figures to persuade audiences to either accept or reject certain ideas, initiatives, and agendas. In *Politicians and Rhetoric: The Persuasive Power of Metaphor* (2011), author Jonathan Charteris-Black examines former political figures such as George W. Bush and Martin Luther King Jr., observing how often they used metaphoric framing in their speeches to help audiences understand and, more importantly, to accept their political views. As one example, Bush used the persuasive tactic of metaphoric framing following the 9/11 attacks, where he dehumanized terrorists by conceptualizing them in terms of animals, vermin, and insects.

> Initially, the terrorists may *burrow deeper into caves* and other entrenched hiding places. (7 October 2001)
>
> It's an enemy that likes to *hide and burrow* in and their network is extensive...But we are going to *smoke them out.* (17 September 2001)
>
> We will not allow ourselves to be terrorized by somebody who thinks they can hit and *hide in some cage* somewhere...to get them running and to find and to *hunt them down.*
>
> (Charteris-Black, 2011, p. 264)

By framing terrorists as wild and dangerous animals, Bush "implied that they have forsaken any claim to be treated like human beings" (Charteris-Black, 2011, p. 264). Because metaphoric framing has the power to define certain ideas (terrorists are animals), the power of metaphoric framing should not be overlooked. Take, for instance, the treatment of Jews during World War II. "It was only by thinking of Jews *as if* they were animals or insects that permitted those in charge of following instructions to implement the policy of the Final Solution" (Charteris-Black, 2011, p. 266). Using graphic, intense, and dramatic metaphors to frame concepts can have serious and even dangerous consequences, and, historically, the power of metaphoric framing has had significant impact.

This, then, is how we usually understand metaphor. Metaphor is usually understood as a figure of speech. Sometimes it is seen as pure ornament. Other times it is seen as doing something more, like linguistically connecting and transferring meaning across unlike ideas, or like tapping into people's ability to visualize and respond emotionally and be persuaded. Taking some time here in this first chapter to reflect on this common understanding is important because it provides a foundation for comparison—a comparison of this common understanding with an understanding of metaphor as something far more fundamental to human thought and, by extension, human action. And by yet further extension, humans acting.

References

Albala, K. (2014). Shakespeare's culinary metaphors: A practical approach. *Shakespeare's Studies*, *42*, 63–74.

Charteris-Black, J. (2011). *Politicians and Rhetoric: The Persuasive Power of Metaphor*. Palgrave Macmillan.

Dolan, N. (2002). Shylock in love: Economic metaphors in Shakespeare's sonnets. *Raritan*, *22*(2), 26–51.

Fairhurst, G. T., & Sarr, R. A. (1996). *The Art of Framing: Managing the Language of Leadership*. Jossey-Bass Publishers.

Lewis, R. (2012). Hamlet, metaphor, and memory. *Studies in Philology*, *109*(5), 609–641. https://doi.org/10.1353/SIP.2012.0041

Lydon, M. (2010). The power of metaphor. *Thinkmap Visual Thesaurus*. Retrieved from www.visualthesaurus.com/cm/wc/the-power-of-metaphor/

Metaphor. (n.d.) In *Oxford English dictionary online*. Retrieved from www.oed.com

Septianto, F., Pontes, N., & Tjiptono, F. (2021). The persuasiveness of metaphor in advertising. *Psychology & Marketing*, *39*(5), 951–961.

Shakespeare W. 1601. *As You Like It*. Project Gutenberg E-text of *As You Like It* by Shakespeare. www.gutenberg.org/cache/epub/1121/pg1121-images.html (accessed 10 March 2021).

Steuter, E., & Wills, D. (2009) *At War with Metaphor: Media, Propaganda, and Racism in the War on Terror*. Rowman and Littlefield.

Sullivan, K., & Bandin, E. (2014). Censoring metaphors in translation: Shakespeare's *Hamlet* under Franco. *Cognitive Linguistics*, *25*(2), 177–202.

Thompson, A., & Thompson, J. O. (1987). *Shakespeare: Meaning and Metaphor*. Harvester Press.

Valenzano, J. M. III, & Braden, S. W. (2015). *The Speaker: The Practice and Tradition of Public Speaking* (3rd ed.). Fountainhead Press.

2 Metaphor as a way of thinking

As we have shown, metaphor can be used artistically and creatively to embellish language. It can also be used to make connections that extend our understanding or that frame ideas in vivid, compelling ways that assist with our efforts to persuade. People by and large understand and accept these ideas of metaphor, so now it is time to move on to something different—a newer way of understanding metaphor that suggests it is something grander and more powerful than most typically realize.

Metaphor and our conceptual system

It can be and has been argued that metaphor functions as the very foundation of our conceptual system. Lakoff and Johnson's (1980) influential book, *Metaphors We Live By*, played a substantial role in shifting the understanding of metaphor from something we employ to think about present concepts in new ways, to something that actually structures our fundamental understanding of those concepts to begin with. Where metaphor was once viewed as a tool to decorate language or clarify ideas, Lakoff and Johnson suggest that metaphor is the basis of our conceptual understanding. In other words, everything we do, see, say, and experience is based in metaphor, and without metaphor we wouldn't be able to comprehend, explain, and participate in the world around us. Metaphor is "the very foundation of how we think, act, and live" (Lakoff & Johnson, 1980, p. 3).

Lakoff and Johnson use the term "conceptual metaphor" when referencing this particular understanding. In doing so, they

DOI: 10.4324/9781003341024-3

are emphasizing how every thought and all that is part of the conceptualization process is grounded in metaphor. The idea of conceptual metaphor as presented by Lakoff and Johnson is more complex, more multilayered, more expansive than the common understanding of metaphor as a figure of speech or framing tool for persuasion. Even so, we do not believe actors and directors interested in our character analysis method would need to familiarize themselves fully with Lakoff and Johnson's ideas. At the same time, we think their book, *Metaphor's We Live By*, is fascinating and also quite accessible. In our own experiences dealing with this material in the college classroom, we have seen that students often start by wondering how anyone could spend an entire semester exploring something as simple and straightforward as metaphor (which they assume to be a comparison of two unlike things without using the words "like" or "as"), then they begin to read and think and find it strange and a little confusing, and then they start to really "get it" and want to know and understand more, and then they start to report that they are hearing and seeing metaphor everywhere and all the time. Some have said that an introduction to conceptual metaphor and the ideas of Lakoff and Johnson fundamentally changes the way they experience the world.

If you are intrigued, you might decide to find yourself a copy Lakoff and Johnson's book and read it. We think you will be enriched for the experience. However, that is not necessary. A general understanding of some essential ideas and terms will be enough of a foundation for you to appreciate and apply the idea of structural metaphor as the basis for character analysis. What follows, then, is an overview of some relevant terminology.

Source domains, target domains, and metaphoric entailments

A metaphor is a kind of comparison—a comparison of two things that are not considered similar. If I say, "That birthday party was an absolute train wreck!" I am obviously comparing two things: something normally considered a fun and enjoyable celebration, and a tragic event filled with damage and likely injury that no one would want to experience. Of these two things, I am trying to bring attention, clarification, and meaning to one thing—in this case, the birthday party. I am doing that by drawing on people's understanding of and experience with (hopefully not personal experience, in this case) the second thing—a train wreck.

So, we can say that all metaphors are composed of two parts: the concept that needs further clarification, and the concept used to create a more extended understanding. In discussing conceptual metaphor, Lakoff and Johnson refer to these two parts as "domains." There is a "target" domain and a "source" domain. In introducing Lakoff and Johnson's ideas, Kövecses (2010) distinguishes between these two domains as follows:

> The two domains that participate in conceptual metaphor have special names. The conceptual domain from which we draw metaphorical expressions to understand another conceptual domain is called **source domain**, while the conceptual domain that is understood this way is the **target domain**.
>
> (p. 4)

Sullivan (2013) extends this distinction by noting that target and source domains usually differ in regard to how concrete or abstract they are.

> A metaphor is a cognitive process that allows one domain of experience, the target domain, to be reasoned about in terms of another, the source domain. The target domain is usually an abstract concept such as LIFE, whereas the source domain is typically a more concrete concept, such as a DAY. The metaphor allows us to export conceptual structure about the more concrete domain to the more abstract target domain.
>
> (p. 1)

If we were to consider the statement above, "That birthday party was an absolute train wreck!" we can see that "train wreck" fits Kövecses' definition of a source domain; we are drawing on this domain in order to understand something about a particular birthday party experience. "Birthday party," then, is the target domain in this case. When it comes to birthday parties and train wrecks, however, it might be difficult to determine which domain is more concrete and which is more abstract. This difficulty suggests that the expression in question is likely not functioning at the level of a conceptual metaphor and is, instead, a fairly simple linguistic comparison made to bring dramatic emphasis to some negative aspects of a birthday party gone wrong. To further clarify these ideas of target domain and source domain, then, we will focus instead on the metaphoric expression, "Life is a journey."

A great deal of everyday language reflects how thoroughly we tend to understand life as a journey. Kövecses (2010) aptly points out how we commonly refer to getting "a good start" in life, or how we talk about people who "go through a stage" or who "get to the end of the road" in their lives. We also talk about people who are "without direction" or "at a crossroads" in life (p. 3). This way of talking about life is so common and so natural that it probably isn't even thought of as metaphorical at all. Many would argue that life is not "like" something we start, go through, and get to the end of, but that it "is" something we start, go through, and get to the end of.

And that is exactly the point.

Everyday language reveals how, for many, many people—and certainly for those English speakers whose language tradition includes these common expressions—an understanding of life is fundamentally grounded in and structured by an understanding of a journey. Whether we ever think or say the expression, "Life is a journey," our everyday language reveals that, in fact, for us it is.

The metaphoric connections between life and journey go far beyond the basic idea of an event that is started, experienced, and ultimately ended. This is the way of cognitive metaphor. It structures our thinking in systematic ways. A journey is a complexly structured system of ideas, and those ideas can by extension map onto "life" in a way that results in a similarly complex and structured system of understanding. For example, journeys typically involve travelers. So then, in life, we (people) are travelers. Travelers on journeys often are joined by fellow travelers or companions. Our friends in life are understood as our traveling companions for this journey. Those who offer advice and "direction" are the guides for our journey. Events we experience in life are the journey's adventures, side trips, or excursions—or maybe distractions from the journey's path or times when we become a bit lost. Birth and death are, of course, the start and end of our life journey. These are but a sample of the more specific ways we can and do think about and talk about life as a journey. There is a rich, extensive system of ideas that make up the notion of a journey, and this system then provides a powerful and necessary structure for us to conceptualize this amazing, complex, ineffable thing we call life.

Before moving on—by the way, "moving on" is a good example of how virtually everything we say and think is grounded in metaphor. The flow of ideas in a book like this ("flow" of ideas is yet another metaphor) is not "movement" in any real, physical sense. But we do tend to think about the presentation of idea then idea then idea as a kind of motion. Maybe a "flow" like water. But we digress.

Before moving on to more clarification of how conceptual metaphor connects source and target domains in complex, systematic ways, we want to return again to the "That birthday party was an absolute train wreck!" expression referenced earlier. Recall that we presented this expression as a kind of metaphor. It does show how a source domain (a train wreck) can be used to provide some insight into a target domain (birthday party). We also suggested that this expression really does not function as a true conceptual metaphor, and this point can be more fully demonstrated now.

Compare "That birthday party was an absolute train wreck!" with "Life is a journey." We have just shown how our understanding of life is wholistically structured through connection to a rich and elaborate and complex and systematic set of ideas tied to our understanding of journey. The same could never be said of the way that "train wreck" impacts our understanding of "birthday party." Sure, train wrecks include bad, unexpected, chaotic things happening, and it may be that a certain birthday party experience unfortunately came with some bad, unexpected chaos. However, where do we go from there? Train wrecks usually include injured passengers or cargo. Perhaps we could be suggesting that the birthday party attendees are these passengers or cargo, but that association really does not seem evident or clearly intuitive. Train wrecks have causes, such as something on the track or a mechanical failure. Perhaps the birthday party chaos could be attributed to a specific something or someone, but maybe not. Trains run on tracks. Is there something about the birthday party understood as a kind of track? Emergency responders of some sort usually show up to deal with train wrecks. Who might the emergency responders be for birthday party chaos? A person could get creative with all of this and try to force some connections between train wreck and birthday party, but the connections would be just that. Forced. It is highly unlikely that anyone would naturally, inherently draw on the idea of a train wreck and its extended system of associations for a fundamental understanding of a birthday experience.

The point is that some metaphoric expressions are simply ways to emphasize, dramatize, or draw attention to an aspect of one thing by comparing it to another thing. Conceptual metaphor does more. It draws on a coherent system of ideas from one domain to structure a similarly coherent system for conceptualizing another domain. The sets of "systematic correspondences between the source and the target" (Kövecses, 2010, p. 7) domains are known as mappings. This idea of mappings is not unlike the more common understanding of a mapping—for example, a road map. The common road map has many elements: visual representations of actual roads, towns, borders, perhaps lakes and rivers and mountain ranges. Each of these elements systematically corresponds to an element in the physical world. Just as a road map provides an understanding of the physical world across which we desire to travel, the elements of a metaphoric source domain correspond to elements of a target domain and provide a systematic understanding of that target domain.

Road maps are powerful things. Often, they are filled with many visual elements, and each element corresponds to and gives understanding and insight into something in our physical world. However, a road map is also limited since it can only give us understanding and insight about a particular set of elements in our physical world—that is, only those elements in our physical world that have a correspondence to something specifically included in the map. If a road map does not include visual representation of, say, the locations of free public parking spaces, then it will not be helpful for someone looking for free public parking. One would need a different map for this unique purpose.

Conceptual metaphors, unlike road maps, can and often do offer more than meets the eye. The mappings provided by conceptual metaphors are not limited to some predetermined set of correspondences. You could say that the correspondences between source and target domains are possibilities that emerge as needed. Some correspondences may seem obvious—for example, if life is a journey then we are the travelers, birth is the start of the journey, death is the end. But the source domain "journey" offers great potential for additional correspondences to the target domain "life." We have already mentioned some of these such as friends and family being traveling companions, and events in life being excursions, and those who instruct and offering advice being the guides of our journey. But there is so much more, virtually unlimited metaphoric possibility here. As part of our life journey, significant advances in a relationship can be understood as the crossing of a substantial distance, leading us to say something like, "We have come so far together." Conversely, people in a relationship who perceive a lack of interpersonal progression may feel the relationship is "not going anywhere," which may ultimately lead to relational breakup which could be understood as travelers "going our/their separate ways." Additionally, certain kinds of life experiences can be understood as journeying via various forms of transportation ("I feel my life has been completely derailed!") or over various types of terrain ("This last year has been a really long, bumpy road!") or at various speeds ("My life is just creeping along!"). To make plans for my life is to "map out my future," and when I put those plans into action I will hope I am "on the right path," though I know at some point I may need a "course correction."

As a way to emphasize the wonderful, expanding, generative potential for the correspondences between source and target domains, the mappings of conceptual metaphor are referred to as entailments. The word, entailment, relates to the idea of deduction, of predication, of implication—all kinds of extensions. And extension is exactly what conceptual metaphor allows. This extension, taking place through entailments, is the conceptual power metaphor. According to Kövecses (2010), metaphoric entailments are produced "when rich additional knowledge about a source is mapped onto a target" (p. 122). Entailments emerge when aspects of the target domain are elaborated on or extended upon through the use of the source domain. Remember that, most often, we are drawing on something tangible and known (source domain) to better understand something less tangible and unfamiliar (target domain). Conceptual metaphor has the power to uncover "rich additional knowledge" of that less tangible and unfamiliar thing because of the entailments that emerge.

Entailments, then, can be understood as a kind of living, evolving bridge, stretching out and connecting our understanding of an abstract concept to something more familiar, and expanding that understanding through the emergence of more and more points of connection. And, yes, we are fully aware that we are using metaphor (entailments are a kind of living, evolving bridge) to help explain something about how metaphor works. If it is true that metaphor is the very foundation of human conceptualization and understanding, how could we do anything else?

How conceptual metaphor affects thought and action

To this point in the chapter, we have focused on the idea of "life as a journey" to clarify the role of target and source domains, mappings, and entailments in the conceptual metaphor process, a process whereby our understanding of the abstract concept of life is structured by our experience with and understanding of a journey. Lakoff and Johnson (1980) suggest, however, that conceptual metaphor does more than structure thought. It also structures action.

For many, making the connection between thought and action probably seems rather obvious and intuitive, and the claim that how I think about something will impact how I act in regard to that thing may not need explanation or support. However, the approach to character analysis suggested in this book is founded on the notion that what we will be calling structural metaphor can systematically shape an actor's thoughts and that, in turn, those thoughts can guide the actor's dramatic action choices related to character presentation. Because of this, we feel the need to address, at least briefly, this issue of the relationship between thought and action as they relate to metaphor.

In order to clarify the relationship between thoughts and actions, we need to consider our use of language. One reason for this is that "thoughts" are anything but tangible. We can't really point to a thought or see a thought as it is happening. Language, though, is tangible and observable, and language is also directly tied to thought. In their book exploring the metaphorical implications of the "war on terror," Steuter and Wills (2009) make the following observation about the need to examine language to understand the relationship between thought and action as part of our conceptual system.

> Since the way we communicate emerges from the same conceptual systems out of which we think and act, an examination

> of our language becomes especially crucial in analyzing and interpreting that system.
>
> (p. 7)

Therefore, to understand how we think about a concept and how those thoughts relate to how we act in relation to that concept, we must first examine the language in relation to the concept.

Fortunately, we can return to Lakoff and Johnson (1980) themselves for an informative illustration. Here, we see another example of an idea metaphorically wrapped up in the framework of war—in this case not a war on terror but, instead, "argument" as war. Lakoff and Johnson offer examples from everyday language that illustrate how thoroughly most people understand and talk about the process of argument as war.

> ARGUMENT IS WAR
> Your claims are *indefensible*.
> He *attacked every weak point* in my *argument*.
> His criticisms were *right on target*.
> I *demolished* his argument.
> I've never *won* an argument with him.
> You disagree? Okay, *shoot*!
> If you use that *strategy*, he'll *wipe you out*.
> He *shot down* all of my arguments.
>
> (p. 4)

In this example, Lakoff and Johnson show ways in which the source domain (war) is applied to the target domain (argument) "to structure (at least in part) what we do and how we understand what we are doing when we argue" (p. 5). Please notice the claim that the power of this metaphor is in the structuring of "what we do" as well as in the structuring of our understanding. The important point is that "we don't just talk about argument in terms of war" (p. 4), but we also act on our conceptual understanding by attacking and defending positions and by using strategy to plan new lines of attack.

If this example is not enough to convince you that metaphor can shape not only how we think and talk about something but also how we act, take a moment to reflect on your own personal experiences with arguments. Consider arguments you have witnessed and in which you have participated. Many and probably most people would describe being in an argument as an unpleasant, stressful experience—an experience to be avoided and one that likely is accompanied by a racing heartbeat, maybe a dry mouth, increased focus, tightening muscles, and other physiological symptoms characteristic of a seriously threatening situation. An argument often triggers a fight-or-flight response. It may not be an actual combat situation, but it likely feels in many ways similar to what one imagines of a combat situation. As illustrated above, people commonly talk about arguments in combat terms. People talk about being "attacked" in an argument. And this is not simply figurative language for the purpose of emphasis. Some so fully understand and act out argument as war that an exchange of verbal disagreement can at some point transition to physical attack, and that transition can seem like a quite natural extension of the engagement. Even if an argument stops short of physical altercation, individuals who feel they have been seriously verbally attacked in an argument may claim that they have been sufficiently threatened or even injured to warrant legal action. It is clear that argument is not only thought of and talked about as combat and as war—it is in very real and felt ways acted out and experienced as such.

Perhaps, though, the reason people experience argument in this way is because it is fundamentally combative. We suggested earlier that some people might claim that life is not "like" a journey, it "is" a journey. In a similar way, some might claim that arguments are not combative "like" war, they are simply and inherently combative things. Perhaps. But we suggest otherwise. For one thing, we know from experience that there are ways to think about, talk about, and engage in argument-like behaviors that shape the experience quite differently. For example, those who participate in competitive debate are without a doubt engaged in argument. Some may think about, talk about, and experience it as combat and as war, but personal experience in the activity leads us to recognize that many competitive debaters view the experience in highly positive ways—like an enjoyable and challenging game or like a fun sporting event. Competitive but not combative. Not threatening or negative, and certainly not war. The work of diplomacy is also filled with argument-like exchanges. But diplomacy is a strategy often taken specifically to avoid combat or war, and therefore the way diplomacy is thought about and talked about intentionally steers clear of combat or war framing.

What if, in our inherited language tradition, argument was commonly framed not as combative but as a more pleasant kind of engagement like a sporting event or friendly game? Or how about an even more cooperative activity—perhaps as a dance? Could those involved be understood not as enemies or opponents but as partners? Could the outcome not be victory or defeat, a win or a loss, but instead some lovely outcome reflecting engaged, collective human effort and ingenuity worthy of our attention and maybe even applause? Could a really good argument be cause for a standing ovation? Are we taking this possibility a little too far to be realistic? Perhaps. But, again, we suggest otherwise. We are convinced that metaphors are powerful. They provide frameworks for thinking about and talking about things that can and will influence how we act in relation to those things: our lives, our response to international terrorist threats, arguments.

We are far from alone in this. Lakoff and Johnson (1980), along with the many, many others inspired by their work, also contend that "the human conceptual system is metaphorically structured and defined" and "human thought processes are largely metaphorical" (p. 6). They also contend that "metaphor is not merely in the words we use" (p. 5) and that it is not just a fancy way to embellish language, draw comparisons, or frame ideas. As the basis of understanding, the metaphors we use in everyday language are much more than simple figures of speech. Metaphors establish relationships between source domains and target domains, allowing the emergence of systems of entailments, guiding all thought and, therefore, all action.

References

Kövecses, Z. (2010). *Metaphor: A Practical Introduction* (2nd ed.). Oxford University Press.

Lakoff, G., & Johnson, M. (1980). *Metaphors We Live By*. University of Chicago Press.

Steuter, E., & Wills, D. (2009). *At War with Metaphor: Media, Propaganda, and Racism in the War on Terror*. Rowman and Littlefield.

Sullivan, K. (2013). *Frames and Constructions in Metaphoric Language*. John Benjamins. https://doi.org/10.1075/cal.14

3 Structural metaphor

We hope our introduction to some ideas proposed by Lakoff and Johnson (1980) has helped you grasp and more fully appreciate the idea of metaphor as something far beyond ornament or emphasis. Metaphor, it has been argued, is the very basis of human thought and action. If you see this claim as reasonable, and perhaps even compelling, then it should not be asking too much to invite you to consider how conceptual metaphor could provide the foundation for a particularly valuable approach to character analysis. We will share such an approach later in this book. In preparation for that, however, we first need to introduce some additional ideas from Lakoff and Johnson. The reason for this is because there are various types of conceptual metaphors, and the character analysis approach we will be proposing utilizes one specific type: structural metaphor. In order to appreciate the unique utility of our character analysis technique, it is important that you understand both what structural metaphor is and what it is not.

Orientational, ontological, and structural metaphor

Lakoff and Johnson (1980) distinguish among three types of conceptual metaphors: orientational, ontological, and structural. All three are fundamental components to our conceptual metaphoric systems. In particular, orientational and ontological metaphors help us to identify, quantify, and categorize our experiences in terms of spatial orientations, entities, or substances. In other words,

DOI: 10.4324/9781003341024-4

orientational and ontological metaphors frame our understanding in terms of where something is as well as in terms of what something is, including what that something is made of.

Orientational metaphors are grounded in understood characteristics of our embodied, three-dimensional, physical experience. Orientational metaphors project tangible characteristics of our experience onto something less tangible, usually something less physical and less accessible through direct physical perception. Recall the explanation of source domain and target domain in the previous chapter. In light of that explanation, we can say that, for orientational metaphors, our embodied physical experience is the source domain. We know and understand this experience because we have lived it and felt it. For example, because of our embodied, three-dimensional existence, we experientially understand what it means to be physically "up" or "down" in relation to something or someone else. Similarly, we have experienced being "in front of" or "behind" something or someone else. With orientational metaphors, some characteristics of our known, embodied physical experience are projected onto the target domain which is some less physical and more nebulous thing—a nebulous thing such as a "quality" or a "state" or a "disposition" or a "feeling."

As explained by Lakoff and Johnson (1980), orientational metaphors map a series of spatial orientational source domains, such as "up-down, in-out, front-back, on-off, deep-shallow, central-peripheral" (p. 4), onto target domains to "organize a whole series of concepts in terms of another" (p. 14). Examples of orientational metaphors can be seen in the following:

MORE IS UP; LESS IS DOWN: Speak *up,* please. Keep your voice *down,* please.
HEALTHY IS UP; SICK IS DOWN: Lazarus *rose* from dead. He *fell ill.*

CONSCIOUS IS UP; UNCONSCIUS IS DOWN: Wake *up*. He *sank* into a coma.

CONTROL IS UP; LACK OF CONTROL IS DOWN: I'm *on top* of the situation. He is *under* my control.

HAPPY IS UP; SAD IS DOWN: I'm feeling *up* today. He's really *low* these days.

> VIRTUE IS UP; LACK OF VIRTUE IS DOWN: She's an *upstanding* citizen. That was a *low-down* thing to do.
>
> RATIONAL IS UP; NONRATIONAL IS DOWN: The discussion *fell* to an emotional level. He couldn't *rise above* his emotions.
>
> (Kövecses, 2010, p. 40)

In these metaphors, we can see that reference to an upward orientation drawn from an "up-down" source domain elicits certain target domain characteristics: more, healthy, conscious, etc. On the flipside, reference to a downward orientation drawn from that same "up-down" source domain elicits quite different target domain characteristics: less, sick, unconscious, etc. Overall, it appears that the spatial orientation of up is characterized as positive, while the spatial orientation of down is characterized as negative. However, this general pattern of "up" being positive and "down" negative should not be understood as somehow universal or inherent. Lakoff and Johnson (1980) observe that orientational metaphors "are rooted in our physical and cultural experience" (p. 18). Arguing that they are rooted in our physical experience might imply some kind of universality given that the laws of the physical world are consistent from person to person across time and space, at least as we experience those physical laws. On the other hand, recognizing that these metaphors are also rooted in cultural experience opens the door to the possibility—even the likelihood—that one's personal experience of physical orientation is shaped by culture. Is "upness" universally understood as a more positive thing than "downness"? We tend to think of being "shallow" or "in the back" or "on the periphery" as less positive than their opposites (deep, front, central), but is that true for everyone, everywhere, and throughout time? The answer to these questions is no. Culture as well as direct physical experience provide a foundation for understanding our orientational experiences. Therefore, we can expect there to be variation in the particular ways these experiences serve as orientational metaphor source domains. The point we are making here, though, is simply that, through orientational metaphor, spatial experience does in fact systematically shape our understanding of many other aspects of our world.

Orientational metaphors can provide a valuable basis for understanding; however, as Lakoff and Johnson (1980) themselves noted, "one can only do so much with orientation" (p. 25). It is good, then, that ontological metaphors provide another powerful conceptual tool for understanding and for guiding action in our world. Ontology is the philosophical study of being, existence, and reality. Ontology is driven by the questions "What is it?" or "What is it made of?" It should make sense, then, that ontological metaphors provide frameworks for understanding target domains by drawing on connections to the source domains of substances or entities. An example of an ontological metaphor can be seen in the following:

> INFLATION IS AN ENTITY
> *Inflation is lowering* our standard of living.
> If there's much *more inflation,* we'll never survive.
> We need to *combat inflation.*
> *Inflation is backing* us into a corner.
> *Inflation is taking its toll* at the checkout counter and gas pump.
> Buying land is the best way of *dealing with inflation.*
> *Inflation makes me sick.*
>
> (Lakoff & Johnson, 1980, p. 26)

As is true for most metaphors, ontological metaphors take advantage of something more tangible and recognizable (the source domain) to provide a conceptual framework for something less so (the target domain). In the case of this example, one might question whether something as nonspecific as "an entity" can be considered tangible and recognizable. That would be a fair question. However, even if "entity" is a broad and nonspecific category, it is a broad and nonspecific category of things that are tangible and recognizable. In fact, "something that is tangible and recognizable" could serve as a pretty decent definition of "entity." Conversely, some might argue that "inflation" is pretty tangible and recognizable. It is probably true that the word "inflation" is something with which we are rather familiar. We likely hear it used, perhaps on the news and more so during certain periods of time than others. But truly explaining what inflation "is" would be a real challenge. Based on what we hear on the news, it is a real challenge even for seasoned economists. Inflation is a very complex economic condition, impacted by many, many variables. It certainly would be much easier to point to most any actual "entity" one could think of than it would be to point to "inflation."

Our intention here is not to try to convince anyone of the tangibility or recognizability of an entity. Instead, it is to show how ontological metaphors work. Ontological metaphors help us understand things that generally are not considered substances or entities by referencing them as substances or entities. "Inflation is an entity." "The mind is a storage container" (What do you have *in* mind?). Actually, many activities are understood as containers (e.g., There were a lot of wonderful performances *in* that production!). As Lakoff and Johnson (1980) suggest, ontological metaphors frame an intangible and complex thing in a way that allows us to "refer to it, quantify it, identify a particular aspect of it, see it as a cause, act with respect to it, and perhaps even believe that we understand it" (p. 26).

We hope it is clear that both orientational and ontological metaphors help us to better understand our world. They do so by framing the often ineffable dimensions of the world through the lens of some more tangible aspect of our personal, physical experiences. However, when it comes to the conceptual utility of orientational and ontological metaphors, Lakoff and Johnson (1980) suggest that they "serve a very limited range of purposes—referring, quantifying, etc." (p. 27), and that framing abstract concepts through the metaphoric lens of a spatial orientation, entity, or substance does not allow for many entailments. Recall from the previous chapter that we described entailments as a living and evolving bridge that connects our understanding of an abstract concept to something more familiar. We also suggested that the real power of conceptual metaphor is the potential for extending the entailment connections between source and target domain, allowing us to expand our understanding through the emergence of more and more points of metaphoric connection. We stand behind our claim that the potential for entailments to grow and expand offers "virtually unlimited metaphoric possibility." At the same time, we acknowledge what Lakoff and Johnson are suggesting about the limited purposes of orientational and ontological metaphors. One additional type of metaphor, however, is particularly flexible in its application, and it allows for a particular abundance of extensions or entailments. It is known as structural metaphor.

Similar to orientational and ontological metaphors, structural metaphors are "grounded in systematic correlations within our experience" (Lakoff & Johnson, 1980, p. 61). But unlike orientational and ontological metaphors, structural metaphors allow for more mappings between source and target domain, therefore producing more entailments. As an example of a structural metaphor, consider the idea of "the mind as a machine." In this example, tangible aspects of a machine can be mapped onto the more abstract concept of the mind. This mapping allows for the creation of a vast system of entailments.

For instance, if the mind is a machine, then we can understand things we learn, that is "information," as data that "comes into" the mind. We likely think of memory as the "part" of the mind-machine that "stores" information or data. As a machine, the mind may then "process" that data or "organize" it. This processing and organizing includes "transmitting" or "sending" information from one part of the machine to another. Sometimes, we want to keep particular information "at the front" of our mind, and at other times we may choose to move something to "the back of" our mind. Thinking, therefore, is ultimately understood as the active functioning of this mind-machine. When we are thinking, the mind-machine is on. When we are given a mental task and someone asks us if we have come up with a solution, we might say, "I'm working on it!" Sometimes, when we just can't stop our mind-machine from thinking-working, we might "wish we could turn our mind off," or if our mind-machine is "stuck" on something in particular, we might complain that, "I just can't get it out of my mind!" All of this receiving and processing and organizing and storing and transmitting information can be a lot for one mind-machine to handle. We know that sometimes a machine like a dishwasher or a table saw or a computer printer can be pushed too far and can break down. We also know that sometimes too much mind-machine work can cause one to have a mental "breakdown."

Hopefully, you can see how possible it is to transfer detailed aspects of the machine source domain (types, parts, process, etc.) onto the mind target domain. The metaphoric connections suggested in the paragraph above are only the tip of the iceberg in terms of possible entailments here. The power of structural metaphor is in the way it allows the target domain to be explored in "considerable detail" (Lakoff & Johnson, 1980, p. 61).

Now, as we have been introducing this third type of conceptual metaphor, you may have noticed something that could be a bit confusing. We have been using the idea of "the mind as a machine" as an example of structural metaphor and how structural metaphors have such rich potential for expanding entailments. It would not be surprising if, along the way, you have wondered to yourself, "But isn't a machine an 'entity'? If so, wouldn't framing the mind as a machine be an example of an ontological metaphor? In fact, didn't they just a bit earlier present 'The mind is a storage container' specifically as an example of an ontological metaphor?"

If you have been wondering such things, we first of all would respond with, "Well done!" Questions like these would suggest that, as a reader, you are really getting this, and that is no small accomplishment. We would also respond by letting you know that, in fact, yes, you are correct. Understanding the mind as a machine is a kind of ontological metaphor. And we might also remind you of some other examples of "mind as a machine" entailments—examples such as keeping information "at the front" of our mind or moving something to "the back of" our mind. These examples are consistent with the idea of the mind as an entity, specifically some kind of information container. They also are suggesting something about the location (front, back) of information within the mind entity. A location is a spatial orientation. Is the "mind as a machine" metaphor, then, also a kind of orientational metaphor? We think you have very good grounds to make that argument.

If the idea of "the mind as a machine" can be understood as an orientational metaphor, and as an ontological metaphor, why would we be presenting it as an example of this third kind of metaphor…a structural metaphor…the kind of conceptual metaphor that has such potential for extended mapping and entailments? Why would we do that?

In actuality, the lines between these types of conceptual metaphors are not so clear. For example, if something is to be understood in terms of its location or orientation, it pretty much has to also be understood as some kind of entity since spatial orientations are characteristics of things (i.e., entities) in physical relationship. While Lakoff and Johnson do make distinct reference to orientational, ontological, and structural metaphors, they present structural metaphors not so much as a third type of conceptual metaphor, but instead as a conceptual metaphor—be it orientational or ontological—with that wonderful power for identifying more and more entailments and for, as we already claimed, virtually unlimited metaphoric possibility. It might be better to suggest that structural metaphor is not actually a metaphor type but, instead, an important metaphor quality. A conceptual metaphor on steroids. A conceptual metaphor that has tapped into its full potential. As Lakoff and Johnson (1980) explain, "structural metaphors provide the richest source of elaboration" and "allow us to do much more than just orient concepts, refer to them, quantify them, etc., as we do with simple orientational and ontological metaphor; they allow us, in addition, to use one highly structured and clearly delineated concept to structure another" (p. 61). Through the associations offered by structural metaphor, more mappings and entailments can occur, and these entailments provide further exploration and understanding of the concept in question.

Gareth Morgan's application of structural metaphor

In *Images of Organization*, Gareth Morgan (1997) draws on this power of structural metaphors to explore aspects of organizational life. Morgan explicitly grounds his work in the ideas of Lakoff and Johnson, suggesting that metaphor can be used to understand, connect with, and function in the world around us. "The use of metaphor implies *a way of thinking* and *a way of seeing* that pervade how we understand our world generally" (Morgan, 1997, p. 4). The particular part of the world Morgan is most interested in thinking about and seeing is the modern organization.

In his book, Morgan applies a number of structural metaphors to organizational life. Each chapter is dedicated to exploring the powerful potential for conceptual insight of a distinct structural metaphor: the organization as a "machine," the organization as an "organism," the organization as a "culture," the organization as a "brain," the organization as a "political system," etc. We know from Lakoff and Johnson (1980) that structural metaphors function by projecting the characteristics of one structural experience onto another. Therefore, a structurally complex concept such as a machine (source domain) can be transferred onto another structurally complex concept such as an organization (target domain).

Though each chapter in his book is dedicated to illustrating the potential of one specific structural metaphor, Morgan ultimately reveals the value of exploring "the implications of different metaphors when thinking about the nature of organizations" (Morgan, 1997, p. 6). Through applying a variety of structural organizational metaphors, Morgan is helping leaders to discover new ways of seeing and dealing with challenging organizational issues. The more complex the issue, the more complexly we need to see it if we are to find helpful ways to respond. What Morgan is suggesting is not unlike the parable of the blind men and the elephant, the story of a group of individuals who are for the first time experiencing a large, complex, unfamiliar beast. Without sight, these individuals must rely on imagining what the elephant is like by touching it. Because of the elephant's great size, each blind man feels a different part of the elephant's body, but only one part, such as the side or the tusk. Individually, each describes what he encounters accurately, but partially. The one touching the elephant's trunk says it is like a serpent. The one touching a leg says, no, it is like a tree. They each describe the elephant based on their limited experience; however, collectively their differing descriptions of the elephant can lead to a fuller and better understanding.

So it is, says Morgan, with organizational life. Each metaphor provides a distinct conceptual framework. Consider, for example, some implications of understanding an organization as a "machine." This is actually a very common metaphoric frame for understanding organizations and organizational life, especially for those living in the post-industrial revolution Western world. Many people would be quite comfortable talking and thinking about the modern Western organization in mechanistic ways. Some might suggest that when an organization is performing properly it is functioning like a "well-oiled machine" or that it is "firing on all cylinders" or that things are "running like clockwork." Others might be struggling for a sense of real purpose or value as an employee and say that they feel they are "just another cog" in the machine. If an organization has experienced serious problems or diminished productivity, there may be a need to do some "reengineering" or to hire a new top leader who can "get the place up and running again." If those efforts don't help things enough, there could be a call to simply "shut the place down."

Overall, the machine metaphor directs us to focus on issues of production, processes, design, consistency, and efficiency. Conversely, one might instead view an organization as a living "organism"—something more like the human body or the environment. Organisms are living systems and, as systems, are like machines to a degree, made up of different pieces that together constitute the whole. However, the pieces of an organism are quite different from the pieces of a machine. For one thing, an organism's pieces—a water source in the environment or the spleen in the human body for example—are far more integrated than the cogs and belts and gears of a machine. When a part in a machine breaks down, it often has no real impact on the rest of the machine. It simply needs to be removed and replaced by another similar part that is non-defective. Even with medical advancements, replacing a spleen is not so easy a task. Nor is replacing a seriously polluted water source or one that no longer exists due to drought. And the impact of that water source, or that spleen, on the entire living system is likely significant and lasting.

Framing organizational life through the lens of an organism, then, might lead us to focus not on consistency and efficiency, but on organizational health and adaptation in response to changes in the larger environment. Employees might be viewed not as replaceable cogs but as essential organs that both depend on and are depended on by the entire organizational body, or as integrated subsystems that must remain vibrant and healthy and in balance with the larger ecosystem. The machine metaphor can draw our attention to certain important aspects of organizational life. The organism metaphor will draw our attention to other also very important things. The elephant is like a serpent. Yes. It is also like a tree.

Morgan's work is a direct application of the work of Lakoff and Johnson. Morgan shows those interested in organizational life how that world can be more fully and richly illuminated through the power of structural metaphor. Morgan argues that changing the metaphor through which you view an organization will lead to new insights and discoveries about that organization. The structural metaphors Morgan presents in his book "are a tool for improving our ability to see, understand, and interpret key aspects of organizational life" (Morgan, 1997, p. 8).

Morgan's work shows us that our understanding of a complex and abstract idea—the idea of a human organization in this case—can be significantly impacted through the power of structural metaphor. Because the source domain (e.g., an organism) of a structural metaphor is complex and systematized, the opportunity for mappings and entailment connections to the target domain (e.g., an organization) is greatly enhanced. Structural metaphors "allow us to do much more than orient concepts, refer to them, quantify them, etc., as we do with simple orientation and ontological metaphors; they allow us to use one highly structured and clearly delineated concept to structure another" (Lakoff & Johnson, 1980, p. 61). Because structural metaphor has proven to be such a beneficial tool for organizational analysis, its ability to provide insight makes it a promising tool for other areas of study.

References

Kövecses, Z. (2010). *Metaphor: A Practical Introduction* (2nd ed.). Oxford University Press.

Lakoff, G., & Johnson, M. (1980). *Metaphors We Live By*. University of Chicago Press.

Morgan, G. (1997). *Images of Organization* (2nd ed.). Sage.

Section II

Metaphor as a tool for character analysis

4 Character analysis and the limitations of ontological metaphor

Character analysis is a rather general term, referencing a broad range of techniques to enhance the actor's craft. Theatrical performers must learn and master some of these techniques to guide them in researching, developing, and assembling the roles which they will portray. That fact is really the basis of this book and the reason we wanted to offer an additional character analysis tool to add to those already available. The importance of such tools is made clear in Charles McGaw's *Acting Is Believing: A Basic Method* (1966). One of many well-established sources for learning character analysis techniques, McGaw's work has withstood the test of time, having resulted in numerous updated editions that have been used in classrooms and training studios over the years to give aspiring actors the tools they need for performance success.

One message that McGaw emphasizes is something anyone reading this book already knows well—that raw talent alone is not enough. As with all arts, acting requires training and the application of proven technique. "Performing a significant role requires both talent and technical skills fully as great as those necessary for a professional pianist to perform a major concerto. This talent can be developed and these skills acquired only through proper training" (McGaw, Stilson, & Clark, 2012, p. 6). McGaw also introduces aspiring actors to the idea that, while some character analysis techniques focus on exploring and developing the external aspects of a character reflected primarily as voice and movement, other techniques focus on exploring and developing what might be called the inner life of the character—dimensions of a character such as thoughts, feelings, motivations, and intentions.

DOI: 10.4324/9781003341024-6

External and internal character analysis

McGaw (1966) suggests that actors start "by discovering the physical life of the character" (p. 5) and "creating a character by making a score of appropriate physical actions, and by carrying them out without attention to [the actor's] own feelings or the feeling of the character [the actor] is creating" (p. 15). This important work provides a solid foundation for the difficult task of digging into the inner life of a character. McGaw's recognition of the distinction between external character analysis and internal character analysis, and his recognition that both are necessary for rich character development, comes as no surprise. McGaw's work is heavily grounded in the ideas and methods of the great Russian born actor and theatre director, Constantin Stanislavski, whose own method is an integration of external and internal character exploration.

There are some who tend to think of Stanislavski's approach as a primarily if not exclusively internal approach to acting. A 2022 article by Jonathan Marshall in the journal, *Stanislavski Studies*, is testimony to this confusion. In his study, Marshall observes that there is a kind of selective understanding when it comes to Stanislavski. According to Marshall, people tend to think of Stanislavski as deeply concerned with the "innovative practice of acting," often assuming, therefore, a focus on the internal dimensions of character. At the same time, Marshall's research revealed that the applied teaching of Stanislavski's techniques often highlights approaches to script analysis as a means for exploring largely external character traits. Regardless of the confusion on the part of some, Stanislavski's method includes an integration of the internal and external. Yes, he grounded his character analysis techniques in detailed and methodical script analysis, a technique that is certainly useful for the discovery of external character traits. However, Stanislavski suggested that actors must first analyze their scripts for "given circumstances, objectives, action, and units of action" (Baron, 2013, p. 31) in order to come to an understanding of the deeper motivations and actions that guide the character's behaviors and decisions.

Another well-known system of character analysis and development was established by theatre practitioner, Uta Hagen. Like so many others, her method was grounded in the work of Stanislavski. In her book, *Respect for Acting* (1973), Hagen identifies two different kinds of actors: the representational and the presentational.

> The Representational actor deliberately chooses to imitate or illustrate the character's behavior. The Presentational actor attempts to reveal human behavior through the use of himself, through an understanding of himself, and consequently an understanding of the character he is portraying.
>
> (p. 12)

It probably is not too difficult to recognize the natural connection between representational acting and external character analysis, and the natural connection between presentational acting and internal character analysis.

Hagen herself did not coin the representational and presentational labels. In fact, she makes it clear that the labels "annoy and confuse" (1973, p. 11) her. Her discussion of representational and presentational actors is primarily a way to indicate her strong preference for the presentational, and, therefore, an emphasis on internal character analysis in her method. Even so, Hagen makes clear that she does "not reject *in toto* the Representational" (p. 13). Her method may not specifically integrate tools for external character analysis, but Hagen certainly recognizes the importance of the external, physical aspects of the actor's art. She states, "Essential to a serious actor is the training and perfecting of the outer instrument—comprising his body, his voice, and his speech" (p. 14).

The point in all of this is simply to acknowledge that, from Stanislavski to Hagen, and then to McGaw and the many, many others influenced by these theatre world greats, those committed to helping actors create robust performances know the importance of tools and techniques for developing both the external and the internal aspects of a character.

Examples of character analysis techniques

There are many external character analysis techniques that focus on the physical and vocal aspects of characterization. McGaw (1966) suggests that actors should engage in a variety of mental and physical exercises in order to help discover and develop the external traits of a character. These might begin with general exercises in relaxation and focus, stretching, guided movement, vocal warmups, etc. Such exercises can help actors to relax, develop body control, and prepare the voice for speaking and the body for moving. More specific strategies that include improvisation or written analysis allow actors to experiment with various voice and movement options. When taking on the task of character analysis, actors can use these kinds of techniques to help in developing external traits needed to better understand and present their character.

Just as there are many approaches to external character analysis, there are many ways to approach the challenging task of internal character analysis. For example, with her "five key elements," famous "nine questions," and various practical acting exercises, Hagen (1973) offers a variety of valuable tools. Hagen suggested that actors focus on their own personal experiences to help create more believable characters. She described two primary ways to work on this presentational style of characterization: emotional recall and sense memory.

For those who may be unfamiliar, emotional recall asks actors to bring very raw, emotional experiences from their own lives into their characterizations. To illustrate, we would like to share a personal example from an experience one of us had as a director. In 2004, Angeline directed a production of *The Shadow Box* and incorporated the emotional recall technique into her rehearsal process. This Tony award winning play follows three separate family units as they deal with the final stages of cancer. The play depends on a level of emotional realism that most of Angeline's actors had not experienced. They spent the first three months of the rehearsal process working through improvisational exercises allowing them to explore emotional experiences from imagined moments in their characters' past, present, and future. These moments were not scripted; instead, they were based on character experiences derived from the actual script references, or they were created through a written character analysis process.

Through an improvisational process, actors were allowed to "live out" moments of deep emotional experience—the kind of emotional experiences relevant to moments referenced in the actual play (e.g., death of spouse, divorce, loss of a child, etc.). When the actors were finally on stage and in performance, they could then recall those improvised moments in order to bring real and raw emotional experiences into their characterization. Angeline's goal in using this improvised emotional recall technique was to help the actors to identify and present on stage realistic and believable character actions and reactions.

Like emotional recall, sense memory relies on a process of recollection. Actors using the sense memory technique are asked to recall specific physical sensations from moments in their own lives and then to incorporate those sensations into their characterization. Through sense memory, actors focus on personal experiences with taste, touch, smell, sound, and sight. Hagen suggests that, by evoking vivid memories of sensory experiences and responses from their own lives (e.g., the smell of an orange), and by incorporating them into their characterization, actors can identify and present more realistic actions and reactions on stage.

Rosary O'Neill's, *The Actor's Checklist* (2007), is another good source that introduces various character analysis techniques. O'Neill follows the ideas of Stanislavski, suggesting that actors should start with the script to focus their character analysis around objective, action, and obstacles. According to O'Neill, actors should search the script for evidence of the desires and motivations that form a character's objectives, clues on achieving those objectives, and any obstacles that might get in the way. Actors engage in this "book work" by spending a significant amount of time searching for textual signs of surface level internal and external character traits. As O'Neill suggests, actors would do well to use the script as the basis for digging deeper and going beyond the text itself, elaborating to create a more extensive character background to "fill the gaps" that might not be apparent in simple script analysis alone.

In this book, we are introducing a new character analysis technique grounded in the idea of structural metaphor. However, metaphor has for some time been the foundation of particular techniques for character exploration. Specifically, ontological metaphor has been used to aid actors in the discovery of external character traits. Recall our earlier discussion of ontological metaphor. Ontological metaphors help answer the questions "What is it?" or "What is it made of?" about a target domain. They do so by referencing source domains that are substances or entities. "Inflation is an entity." "The mind is a storage container."

For some examples of character development exercises based on ontological metaphor, we can again look to *The Actor's Checklist* (2007). In this guide, O'Neill includes familiar exercises such as "playing a giant, acting like an animal, and acting like a machine" (pp. 119–120). Many actors and directors rely on these analysis exercises to aid in the process of discovering external character traits. For instance, through "playing the giant," the actor explores possible character physicalization by embracing large, exaggerated, giant-like behavior, movement, and vocal quality. Through the metaphor "my character is/is like a giant," an actor can physically explore in order to discover parallels or contradictions between the traits of a giant and the traits of the character. Certain vocal or physical traits might then be incorporated into character presentation.

O'Neill (2007) suggests that using the metaphor of an animal or object also could be applied to expand external characterization and lead to a more engaging and compelling performance. "The traits of an animal are graphic and communicate immediately with an audience" (p. 115). Actors and audience members alike can recognize obvious animalistic qualities, and these qualities can affect the way a character is viewed and interpreted. For example, if a character was determined to be "mouse-like," the actor might focus on quick, sharp movements and a quiet or possibly high-pitched and squeaky sounding voice. The expectation would be that audience members would recognize and relate to those "mousy" qualities, leading them to understand and perhaps empathize with the character.

Like the animal metaphor, O'Neill also suggests that actors might apply the metaphor of a machine in order to find a range of rhythmic sounds or movements to incorporate into their characterization. "The traits of a machine can add an exciting dimension to your role" (O'Neill, 2007, p. 121). We know from experience that this technique can be and often is used in introductory acting classes. One specific application is by instructing students to "build" a machine by "attaching" themselves to other actors. As they do, their job is to come up with some kind of improvised mechanical movement and sound. The exercise not only encourages actors to step out of their comfort zones and to work together to create a multi-person machine, it also helps them to experiment with options for movement and sound. If this is being applied for character development, the goal is for actors to find certain physical and vocal qualities that can be usefully incorporated into monologue and scene performance.

There are many ways to approach character analysis. Regardless of the approach an actor chooses, the intended outcome is the same. The results of character analysis should help an audience come to a clearer understanding. In the theatre, "audiences encounter performers' observable actions, and these form a substantial basis for inferences about the meaning and ideological implications of the narrative" (Baron, 2013, p. 33). The application of ontological metaphor has been an important foundation for a variety of valuable character analysis techniques, allowing for creative ways to discover and develop external characterization. It has been and undoubtedly will continue to be a valuable tool for actors.

The limits of ontological metaphor and the promise of structural metaphor

Actors and directors have been relying on the creative power of metaphor to guide character exploration for a long time. However, we think you can see from the examples above that the way metaphor has been applied has primarily if not exclusively focused on assisting in the development of external physicalization and vocalization. This seems to us to be a limitation resulting from the fact that these techniques and exercises apply ontological metaphor. As we noted in the previous chapter, Lakoff and Johnson (1980) argued that ontological metaphors—along with orientational metaphors—are inherently limited. They "serve a very limited range of purposes—referring, quantifying, etc." (p. 27).

For Lakoff and Johnson as cognitive linguists, ontological metaphors are limited in conceptual utility because they do not allow for expansive entailment exploration. For actors and directors interested in the utility of metaphor as a tool for character analysis, the problem is that current techniques are applications of ontological metaphors, and their entailment limitations seem to keep them useful only for exploring aspects of external characterization. These ontological metaphor exercises provide limited insight into the internal aspects of characterization such as interpretation of plotline, character motivation, objectives, and character relationships. The metaphors used in current character analysis techniques can help actors in determining traits related to body position, vocal quality, and character ticks, but they are not as helpful for answering important internal characterization questions like "Who am I?" "Why am I this way?" "Why do I act this way?" "Why do I think these thoughts?" "How do my actions affect the other characters?" "How do my actions affect the action of the play?"

Deep internal and contextual character insights are essential to compelling performances. We are convinced that there are certain kinds of metaphors that have the potential to offer such deep insights. These are structural metaphors, and they can allow actors to go beyond the kind of insight offered by the ontological metaphors typically relied on with existing character analysis techniques. Structural metaphors offer virtually unlimited potential for expanding, extending, and elaborating metaphoric entailments—those interesting and illuminating connections between the thing we are using to help us understand and the thing we want to understand more fully. Not only do we see structural metaphor as a tool for guiding robust individual character development, but we also see it as offering a unifying framework to guide an entire production. Because of this, we committed ourselves to developing an approach to character analysis that capitalizes on the power of structural metaphor. In the following chapters, we want to share that approach and offer some extended examples of how it can be usefully applied.

References

Baron, C. (2013). Stanislavsky's terms for script analysis: Vocabulary for analyzing screen performances. *Journal of Film and Video, 65*(4), 29–41.

Hagen, U. (1973). *Respect for Acting*. Macmillan.

Lakoff, G., & Johnson, M. (1980). *Metaphors We Live By*. University of Chicago Press.

Marshall, J. W. (2022). Outside-in or inside–out? The conflicted discourse of Stanislavski in Australia and Aotearoa New Zealand: part one. *Stanislavski Studies, 10*(1), 9–20. https://doi.org/10.1080/20567790.2021.2011080

McGaw, C. (1966). *Acting Is Believing: A Basic Method* (2nd ed.). Holt, Rinehart, and Winston.

McGaw, C., Stilson, K. L., & Clark, L. D. (2012). *Acting Is Believing* (11th ed.). Wadsworth.

O'Neill, R. (2007). *The Actor's Checklist.* Cengage Learning.

5 Using structural metaphor for character analysis

In light of the work of Lakoff and Johnson (1980), we see structural metaphor as a promising tool for character analysis. Structural metaphor can provide actors a deep understanding of their characters, and their characters' relationship to the broader world of the play. Structural metaphors have this potential due to the way they allow for the creation and extension of elaborate systems of connections—connections we have referred to as entailments—leading to richer understanding and encouraging further inquiry.

Earlier, in Chapter 3, we introduced the work of Gareth Morgan to illustrate the power of structural metaphor as an analysis tool. Morgan (1997) suggests that, when applied to organizational analysis, structural metaphor can lead to "insights and perspectives that will be rather new" and can "generate a range of complementary and competing insights," helping organizational leaders "learn to build on the strengths of different points of view" (p. 6). The method we are proposing here borrows from Morgan's work. It guides actors to see things through the lenses of different structural metaphors, mapping new entailments and leading to new ways of understanding their characters and the relationship of their characters to the broader action of the play.

In the following sections, we offer three examples of how structural metaphors could be used for character analysis. These three metaphors are by no means the only ones that could or should be used in applying our method. We chose these because they have been recognized by Morgan and others as particularly useful for gaining insight into aspects of our complex social world. They are

DOI: 10.4324/9781003341024-7

intended to illustrate the application and utility of our approach. However, if Lakoff and Johnson are correct, then we are swimming in an ocean of powerful metaphors whether we realize it or not. They are there for the taking, and we suggest they are there for the using as tools for character analysis. As a start, let's see what might happen if we look at the action of a play as a machine, as an organism, and as a culture.

The action of the play as a machine

Before we jump in to show how this first metaphor might be applied, we need to address something that could be a point of confusion. We are suggesting here that the "machine" metaphor is a structural metaphor and has real potential to guide rich, in-depth character analysis. However, in the previous chapter, we specifically pointed out how some existing character analysis techniques draw on the idea of the actor as a machine to help identify useful external characteristics for enriching performance. In that discussion, we were pointing out the limitations of the ways metaphor has been applied in character analysis, and we identified the machine metaphor as an example of ontological metaphor—not as a structural metaphor.

So which is it? Is the machine metaphor an ontological metaphor and, thus, quite limited in its entailment possibilities? Or is it a possibility-rich structural metaphor, capable of virtually endless entailment exploration that can guide in-depth character analysis?

The truth is, it is both. Or perhaps it would be better to state that it can be either. The way the machine metaphor typically has been used in character analysis is as an ontological metaphor. As such, the question guiding the metaphoric application is this: "In what ways is my character like a machine?" Usually the question is even narrower than that: "In what ways might my character sound and move like a machine sounds and moves?" Again, we are in no way suggesting that this application of the machine metaphor in character analysis is without value. The use of the machine metaphor as an ontological metaphor, and the application of other ontological metaphors, has substantial value. However, the value seems limited to primarily if not exclusively external character analysis exploration.

How, then, might the machine metaphor be understood and applied as a structural metaphor? As you will see through this chapter, we suggest that the answer is by allowing the metaphor to frame something bigger than the individual character. The heading for this section of the chapter is not "the actor" as a machine but, instead, "the action of the play" as a machine. Therefore, we begin with the proposition that the play itself—all the action of the play in its entirety—is essentially a machine. Then the question for the individual actor becomes, "If the action of the play is a machine, what are the implications for my character?" We think you will see that the implications go far beyond ideas for how a character might sound or move.

As we have indicated, this approach is an extension of what Gareth Morgan suggests for guiding analysis of complex organizational life. Morgan (1997) maintains that viewing organizational life through the metaphoric lens of the machine reveals a "set of mechanical relations" (p. 13) and opens the door to many interesting and valuable insights. Similarly, using structural metaphor and viewing the action of a play as a machine makes possible many interesting and valuable insights for the actor whose character becomes some part of that machine system.

What might be revealed by framing the action of a play as a machine and then considering the implications for a specific character is impossible to predict. That is the beauty and the creative power of structural metaphor. The connections and extensions are virtually limitless. At the same time, most of us are pretty well experienced in thinking of things as machines. For example, Morgan (1997) acknowledges that thinking about organizational life as a machine is extremely common, and for many it seems like the most natural way to understand and talk about one's experience as part of an organization. Consider also how easy it is to think and talk about one's own body as a kind of machine. Even the solar system—made up of parts (planets, moons, etc.) that are connected by gravitational forces and that move in coordinated patterns—can be and has been understood as a sort of perpetual motion machine.

Because of what we know about people's mechanistic framing of things like organizations, bodies, and solar systems, we can expect certain things that would likely come from framing the action of a play as a machine. It seems likely that the result of this metaphoric application would include attention to issues of purpose, efficiency, order, and outcome. Since machines are by definition made up of interconnected parts, we could also imagine attention to the coordination and relationships between and among characters—the parts making up the machine which is the action of the play. But the goal in this character analysis approach is not to go into it with particular expectations. Instead, the idea is to trust in the power of the metaphor—as well as the power of the open imagination of the actor—to lead to interesting and valuable character insights.

As a way to allow actor imagination and ripe metaphor to engage, we suggest beginning by asking a series of broad, overarching questions pertaining to the machine. Consider the following, for example.

If the action of this play is a machine:

- What does the machine do?
- How complex or simple is the machine?
- What might you call/name this machine?
- How efficient and/or effective is the machine at getting the job done?
- Is the machine working properly? What, if anything, is holding the machine back?

Please understand that these are only a few examples. There are no right or wrong questions or prompts here. We are offering some ideas and examples as a way to get started in this character analysis process. Our experience tells us that, once this whole process and the power of structural metaphor is understood, appreciated, and embraced, some rather amazing things can happen. If we thought it was possible to simply provide a specific list of prompts to guide character analysis, there would have been no need for us to offer the earlier chapters. But we do think it is important, even essential, for someone to have a basic introduction to this less common way of understanding metaphor—that is, metaphor as a way of thinking. We believe a foundational understanding of cognitive metaphor, and of structural metaphor specifically, can lead an actor to embrace this technique with real openness and expectation.

In a way, one could argue that developing the kind of understanding and appreciation for structural metaphor that leads to openness and expectation is enough. Abandoning yourself to the power and potential of structural metaphor, engaging with some metaphoric framing of "the action of the play," and allowing the metaphor to take you on a journey into the play and your character—well, that is what we are proposing. However, we know that what we are suggesting here is new and different. Given that, what we want to offer here are at least a few specific examples that could assist someone in initially exploring this approach.

So let us continue, then, with some examples for applying the idea of the action of the play as a machine. Full exploration of this metaphor obviously needs to go beyond the kind of general considerations reflected in the prompts above. For example, actors might want to explore issues related to organization and control of the machine in order to gain insights into aspects of the plot and the roles of other characters. Question prompts such as the following might be useful.

If the action of this play is a machine:

- Who runs the machine?
- What are the most important parts of the machine?
- Are there any parts of the machine that are replaceable?
- What are the different stages or steps that make up the overall process of the machine, and what parts are involved in those steps or stages?

Following consideration of the machine itself, actors might do well to move to more specific questions related to their character's role in the machine.

- What part of the machine am I?
- What do I need in order to function?
- Am I replaceable?
- Do I need work or maintenance?
- How efficient am I currently running?
- How efficient should I be currently running?
- How am I connected to other parts of the machine?

This structural metaphor might also allow actors to explore more internal issues related to personal control, motivation, and relationships to other characters. For example, if an actor determined through metaphor exploration that their character actually controls the machine, they might ask:

- What kind of controller/operator am I?
- Am I part of the machine, such as a handle, a button, or a knob? Or am I an external operator (e.g., an actual person, human operator)?
- What motivation do I have for controlling the machine? Is it purely functional? Do I personally benefit from the functioning of this machine? Am I simply doing what I was designed/destined/paid/ordered to do?
- If I am part of the machine, is another character (or force) "using me" to control the rest of the machine? What does that suggest about my relationship with this machine operator? What does it suggest about my relationship to the other parts of the machine?

Hopefully it is becoming clearer how this kind of metaphoric exploration—the kind that can guide questions of control, self-determination, motivation, and relationships with others—goes beyond considering how one's character might sound or move in machine-like ways. Application of this kind of structural metaphor can allow actors to gain detailed and in-depth character insights.

As Morgan (1997) suggests, the machine metaphor can be compelling. It offers an opportunity to understand some aspect of our world by seeing it as something else—something intentionally designed and constructed to be a systematic whole made up of parts that work together for a purpose or function. Machines are things with which we are familiar and that we generally understand—or at least have a sense that we understand. We can use this sense of understanding and familiarity to gain new insight into something else. For actors, that something else includes the complexities of the action of a play and their character's role in that action.

The action of the play as an organism

A second useful structural metaphor for examining the world of the play and the actor's role within it is the "organism." This is another metaphor presented by Morgan (1997) as being particularly common and particularly useful. In applying the organism metaphor, actors would view the play and the characters as "living systems, existing in a wider environment on which they depend for the satisfaction of various needs" (Morgan, 1997, p. 3). The machine metaphor also relies on looking at the action of the play as a kind of "system"; however, there are actually substantial differences between seeing something as a machine and seeing it as an organism.

First, the machine metaphor conceptualizes something as a "closed system." Closed systems, including machines, are independent from their environments. At least, most machines are designed to be as environment-independent as possible. Consider a common example from the theatre world: the fog machine. A fog machine is a system of sorts. It is made up of many parts and is designed for a particular function. Fog machines exist within environments, of course. But we certainly don't want our fog machine to somehow be sensitive to, to adapt to, to work differently in the stage environment if that environment changes. We don't want the machine to, say, spray more or less fog if the temperature in the theatre goes up or down or if the set is changed between act one and act two. We want the fog machine to, as much as possible, predictably and consistently work the same regardless of its environment.

This is not what we want, need, or expect from organisms. Organisms are "open systems." In fact, they must be or they will not survive. Open systems are defined by their ability to sense, interact with, and adapt to their environment. Perhaps the most familiar organism for most of us is…us. Our physical bodies. We are open systems. As noted earlier, it is a pretty common thing for people to think about their body as a machine. And, in some ways, bodies are machine-like. Bodies are made up of interconnected parts like machines. Bodies seem to be designed for specific purposes. Bodies can be in good working order, but they can also break down when certain parts stop functioning properly. In this day and age, some parts that break down or wear out can even be replaced—not unlike a part on an automobile. Or a fog machine!

But, as we already pointed out, we don't want our fog machine to function differently if it is hot or cold or more or less humid or if the theatre is full for a performance or empty for a rehearsal. Our bodies? That is a different thing entirely. We definitely do want our bodies to function differently if it suddenly becomes very hot or very cold. We need our bodies to sweat so that the evaporation of the sweat cools us down or shiver so the activity warms us up because, at some point, if our body can't regulate its temperature, there will be serious consequences. Potentially, the body could cease to function. That would be bad, and no attempt to replace some faulty parts would be helpful.

We think you get it. Bodies and other organisms are open systems. They have some things in common with closed system machines, but the differences are significant. Those differences mean that viewing the action of a play as an organism is most certainly going to prompt different kinds of connections and insights and implications for character development. For example, where a machine metaphor might draw our attention to issues of production, efficiency, and output, an organism metaphor is more likely to draw out attention to issues of survival, adaptation, and growth. In closed systems, the breakdown of one part often has no ongoing impact on other parts. If the blower fan on a fog machine fails, the machine will not work, but that does not mean the other parts will necessarily also fail. Install a new and functioning blower fan and you are good to go. However, in an organism, the parts of the open, living system very much rely on and affect one another. The greater interconnectedness among parts of an organism means that, if I cut any part of my body and it becomes infected, that could have dire consequences for every other part of my body.

So the organism structural metaphor encourages actors to examine the action of the play as an open and living system, one that can be and will be affected by its external environment and one in which the interconnectedness among the parts means that whatever impacts one impacts all. How and why a character behaves and acts in relation to other characters is always in relation to that character's role in the system of which they are a part. Therefore, in applying this structural metaphor, actors might start by posing a series of broad questions about the nature of the overall living system of the play and the environment in which it exists:

If the action of the play is an organism:

- What kind of organism is it (a human body, a particular animal, a tree or plant, a single living cell, etc.)?
- As an open system, is the organism made up of identifiable subsystems? If so, what are those subsystems and what

characters and other elements of the play make up those subsystems?
- What is this organism's environment? Is the environment "friendly" or "hostile" to the organism?
- What if any changes to the environment take place as part of the action of the play?
- What does the organism most need to survive in this environment?

Following broad consideration of the organism and its environment, actors might do well to move to more specific questions related to how their character is part of the living system.

- What role or roles do I play in helping maintain the organism?
- How do I relate to and affect the other parts of the organism (other characters, etc.), and how do they relate to and affect me?
- When a change in the environment impacts another character as part of the organism, how am I impacted?
- At any point in the action of the play, is my character working to keep the organism healthy, growing, and thriving? If so, why? If not, why not?

When applying the organism metaphor, actors view the play as an open and living system and their character as a part of that living system. Because of that, this perspective can be particularly beneficial as it encourages actors to consider things beyond the boundaries of the play itself—that it, the environment. Thus, this approach might guide actors to more fully and intentionally consider the historical or cultural context within which the action of the play resides. Or, if an actor sees the action of the play as, say, a human body and their character as an organ within that body, then that might help them recognize more clearly what kind of essential function their character performs. It might also help actors to see more clearly how their character and the other characters are inextricably connected and part of a greater whole. This "systems" metaphor would make it virtually impossible for an actor to get overly caught up in their own character, independent from others. Because the parts that make up organisms are so inherently intertwined and interdependent, this metaphoric framing would really bring to light the impact of the actions of the all of the characters.

You have heard the saying, "There are no small parts, only small actors." It seems to us that the organism structural metaphor strongly reinforces this idea. Even the parts of an organism that appear to be small or easy to ignore are, in fact, essential and impactful in the life of the living organism.

The organism structural metaphor offers a framework to guide actors through analysis and exploration of their characters and the plotline "in terms of organic functioning, relations with the environment, relations between species, and the wider ecology" (Morgan, 1997, p. 67). As we have already pointed out, this level of analysis and insight certainly goes beyond revealing possibilities for how a character might move or speak and, instead, can provide actors rich insights into character motivation, desires, and relationships.

The action of the play as a culture

A third structural metaphor that would be useful for guiding actors toward insightful character analysis is the idea of the action of the play as a "culture." When applying this structural metaphor, actors would analyze the play and their character through a cultural metaphoric lens. Like a machine and an organism, a culture is a kind of system. As Morgan (1997) suggests, a culture is "a system of knowledge, ideology, values, laws, and day-to-day rituals" (p. 120).

Despite the fact that a culture can be understood as a kind of system, this metaphor is quite different than that of the machine or organism. One of the most obvious differences is that, with the machine or the organism, the individual character is something other than a person. The character might be a part of machine, like a cog or motor or gear. Or the character might be some piece of an organism, like an arm or a brain or a root system. But the fundamental "pieces" of cultures are people. Thus, of the three structural metaphor examples we are sharing here, this is the first one that asks actors to consider their characters as persons.

Actors might start with questions exploring the nature of the specific culture that makes up the action of the play as well as their character's role within that culture.

If the action of this play is a culture:

- What are the fundamental values and ideals that define my culture?

- Is this culture defined by any specific kind of hierarchy or political system?
- In what ways are the various aspects of the play reflective of the culture. How do different elements of the play serve as cultural artifacts? What action might constitute a cultural ritual? An important symbol? Unique language characteristic? Some important shared cultural knowledge?
- Many cultures have identifiable heroes and/or villains—people who either epitomize cultural values or who live in clear violation of those values. Are there any heroes or villains reflected in the action of the plan?
- Some cultures are very strong and stable and resistant change. But cultures also sometimes go through times of challenge, transition, and even revolution. What is the state of this culture?
- Does the action of the play suggest one unified culture, or are there perhaps multiple cultures or subcultures?
- What are the origins of the values and ideals that make up this culture? Did they seem to primarily emerge from the individuals who are part of the action of this play? Were some things borrowed or adapt from different cultures?

Actors could pose a series of questions focusing more specifically on their own role in the culture.

- What beliefs are at the core of my being, and are these beliefs consistent with the broader culture?
- What role do I play in my culture, and what is that role's cultural significance?
- What is my role in the hierarchy or political system that is part of this culture?
- Am I a cultural hero? A cultural villain?
- What cultural (or countercultural) values guide my actions?
- What day-to-day cultural rituals and routines do I practice?
- Am I part of the mainstream culture, or am I a member of a different culture or subculture?
- How would I answer these questions about all the other characters?

Asking these types of questions clearly digs into the very core beliefs and values that guide a character's thoughts and actions.

Actors would be prompted to explore their own character's value system as well as if and how that might be shared or challenged by other people within in the same culture—that is, within the action of the play. Dramatic conflict is often pretty easy to identify in a play. However, framing that conflict as a larger cultural issue would likely offer different insights and suggest different character choices than framing the conflict as a purely interpersonal or local thing.

Imagine that, through structural metaphor analysis, a certain prop or set piece ended up being identified as an important cultural symbol. As parts of a cultural system, symbols can prompt strong feelings as well as call for certain physical reactions. Identification of such a cultural symbol, therefore, could guide both internal character development (e.g., feelings such as pride, hate, respect) and external character development (e.g., physical responses to cultural symbols such as bowing, kneeling, kissing, pledging). This kind of metaphor exploration might also go beyond impacting individual character development. If it were applied more collectively with an entire cast or production company, it could lead to a director choosing to incorporate certain symbols into stage, prop, lighting, or costume design.

Going beyond one

In his text, Morgan (1997) concedes that, while structural metaphor can be very beneficial in helping to gain new perspectives and insights, there are limitations in the application of any one metaphoric frame. Viewing any complex dimension of human life through a metaphoric lens will cause certain aspects of experience to be emphasized and others to be hidden. For example, seeing something mechanistically and as a closed system brings keen focus on the distinct parts of the system and how those parts function in relation to each other. But as closed systems, machines are designed to have as little relationship or interaction with the environment as possible. A machine metaphoric frame, therefore, discourages consideration of the larger context. This dual emphasizing and hiding capacity is the nature of all metaphor. Morgan refers to the "one-sided insight" offered by metaphor, whereby metaphor has the ability to "highlight certain interpretations and force others into a background role" (p. 4).

When applying this approach to character analysis, then, actors must also concede that a single metaphoric lens will most likely inform and enhance some aspects of characterization while hiding others. For instance, using the structural metaphoric lens of a machine might reveal valuable things related to issues of process, control, and function but distract actors from considering questions of interdependence, growth, or healing, things the organism metaphor might reveal well. However, the organism metaphor could lead to the idea that the purpose of the living system is simply to continue, to not perish, perhaps to grow or heal. That organism focus on simply continuing to live might distract from the possibility that the character or characters of the play functioning as a system may in fact have a more instrumental goal or purpose—a reason for functioning that goes beyond continuing to thrive as a system. The kind of instrumental purpose we usually expect from a machine. And, as already noted, both the machine and living organism metaphors would likely cast the characters as something other than human beings. In doing so, those metaphors tend to make it more difficult to consider the kind of intention and agency that we usually consider the source of human behavior.

We propose, then, that actors should draw from the insights of multiple structural metaphors. In addition, we also want to encourage "going beyond one" by suggesting the value of having multiple actors work together using the same metaphor or set of metaphors. We believe that taking a more collective approach to structural metaphor character analysis has great promise for the richness of a production. Up to this point in this chapter, we have been suggesting some specific prompts for individual actors to use to guide their own individual character analysis. You will see what that might look like more clearly in the two upcoming chapters. But we expect that it is not too difficult to imagine these same prompts for these same metaphors to be considered by an entire cast or even production company. Directors in particular would be in a wonderful position to introduce a cast to the ideas in this book—help a cast to understand, appreciate, and embrace the power of structural metaphor, and then to be guided through considering various metaphors to guide character formation.

This possibility was suggested just a bit earlier, at the end of the section on the action of the play as a culture. We can imagine what might happen if, for example, all members of a cast spent time together in rehearsal discussing possible answers to the culture metaphor prompts: What are the fundamental values and ideals that define our culture? Are any of us cultural heroes or villains? Are we members of a single unified culture or of subcultures? What role does each of us play in this culture? What rituals or symbols can we identify that powerfully reflect cultural values or beliefs? What other ways might we extend this rich metaphor to gain insights helpful to our individual and collective performance?

This kind of collective approach to applying our proposed technique makes intuitive sense given the collective nature of the culture metaphor. However, all three of the structural metaphors we have introduced here are systematic in nature. Machines, organisms, and cultures are all complex systems made up of pieces of some kind. We are confident that any of these three structural metaphors would allow for collective engagement among an entire cast or entire production company, prompting those involved to consider things about the larger system and then also to consider individuals' roles in that system . In fact, because they are defined by their ability to generate rich, interconnected systems of entailments, we will argue that any structural metaphor would have this same potential for collective application. Results of collective engagement with any structural metaphor could prove valuable, perhaps offering a unifying theme or performance structure or visual design guide, as well as allowing for individual actors to get keen insight into both internal and external aspects of their characters. The possibilities are limited only by the imaginations of those involved, and since serious actors and directors and designers in the world of theatre tend to be among the most imaginative people on this planet, we expect that truly wonderful things would happen.

As a way to get started in all of this, consider simply applying the three structural metaphors we have outlined here in this chapter, whether as a personal strategy for your own character analysis or as a broader and more collective approach with an entire cast or company. Do so with a clear understanding that the metaphors of machine, organism, and culture are by no means the only structural metaphors that could be usefully applied, nor are they necessarily the best. In his book, Morgan (1997) offers nine different structural metaphors with which to examine organizational life, and he sees great value in all of them. So, actors and directors, apply multiple structural metaphors. Have some fun, and engage in some serious metaphor play. Consider the power of structural metaphor. Learn to appreciate and respect, and then expect good things. Follow the boundless metaphoric entailments as far as they will take you. By applying multiple structural metaphors, you can "generate a range of complementary and competing insights" that can help you "build on the strengths of different points of view" (Morgan, 1997, p. 6). The more actors have to draw from, the deeper their analysis can be. The deeper and more profound the analysis, the stronger and more compelling the performance. And isn't that what this is all about?

References

Lakoff, G., & Johnson, M. (1980). *Metaphors We Live By*. University of Chicago Press.

Morgan, G. (1997). *Images of Organization* (2nd ed.). Sage.

Section III

Applying the method

6 How this might have worked for Angeline in *The Zoo Story*

Note: This chapter is shared in Angeline's first-person voice.

Some years ago, I appeared in a production of Edward Albee's play, *The Zoo Story* (1993), performing the role of Jerry. I found this show and part to be particularly challenging, and looking back I was not completely satisfied with the outcome. Given that difficulty, I decided the experience would be a good one to draw on for retrospectively applying this structural metaphor technique and exploring how it might have provided deeper and more profound insight into character traits and motivation.

The Zoo Story is a one-act absurdist play that is quite simple in form. The plot centers around two characters, Peter and Jerry.

> Peter, a dull, respectable man with that upper-middle class expression on his face is reading on a park bench when Jerry, an obnoxious stranger, approaches him with irritating personal questions and remarks. The stranger has a desperate need to make contact with someone, and as a last resort pushes his listener to violence.
>
> (Klaus et al., 2002, p. 1036)

The violence at the end of the play is actually a particularly tragic form of suicide. Jerry pulls a knife of Peter, drops the knife so that Peter will pick it up in self-defense, and then Jerry rushes at Peter and impales himself on the knife.

I prepared for this role by conducting initial script analysis. I explored the script in order to determine the preliminary aspects of Jerry's character. In my script analysis, I examined what Jerry had

DOI: 10.4324/9781003341024-9

said about himself, what the playwright had written about Jerry in stage direction, and what others said about him and to him. I also explored his actions as suggested in the script and plot. This initial analysis aided me in understanding base level characteristics and in creating a backstory. These sorts of details can often be inferred from information given in the script, but because some scripts provide limited insight, actors often are given creative freedom to construct their character's history and background.

As an actor, I usually rely on developing backstory to help with motivation and action, allowing me to create moments from the character's past and present that likely will inform both external and internal characterization. For instance, the script didn't provide a lot of detail about Jerry's childhood, a factor that I considered important for providing insight into his motivations and present circumstance. Because childhood is such an important time for the development of emotional, mental, and physical health, along with social and cultural viewpoints, I often try to create a character backstory that includes aspects of my character's childhood. Because the script reveals that, as a character, Jerry has significant issues with intimacy, confidence, and contact, I created a childhood backstory of isolation and abuse.

Although I spent a large amount of time on script analysis, I still had many unanswered questions about why Jerry ends up taking his own life at the end of the play. Ultimately, I struggled with my interpretation and performance. In the following sections, I look back and analyze Jerry through the three structural metaphor lenses of machine, organism, and culture. Through this retroactive analysis, I can see how using structural metaphor could have provided more insight into Jerry's character and helped me answer some of the questions I struggled with during my performance.

The action of the play as a machine

In order to analyze the script and character using this structural metaphor, I posed a series of questions similar to what we suggested in the previous section. "What kind of machine is this? What part of the machine am I? What do I need in order to function? How do I as a part of the machine interact with other parts?"

To determine Jerry's role in the machine, I first had to determine what machine the overall action of the play would be. I reasoned that the machine should be thought of as the thing that propels the motion of the story forward. In this case, I saw the machine as something resembling a vehicle engine. In order to follow this machine metaphor and the entailments that are created through it, I needed to consider an engine's makeup and functioning a bit more thoroughly. In a combustion engine, a combustible material (gasoline) is placed in a small, enclosed area and repeatedly ignited, creating energy in the form of expanding gas. The components of the engine create an ongoing cycle of combustion, allowing this process to occur hundreds of times per minute.

As is true with most machines, the issue of control is such an important factor. A combustion engine only works if the amount of gasoline and air and pressure, as well as the placement and timing of all of this, is carefully controlled. So, as an extension of the structural metaphor of a machine, I had to really examine the extent of Jerry's control. I realized that, while Jerry does have some degree of control, his present circumstances have been externally controlled by years of physical, mental, and emotional abuse, suffered at the hands of his family, his landlady, and by the isolation he experienced throughout his short life. So it made sense to me that the "operator" of this engine, the thing in control, was Jerry's past circumstances. At the same time, Jerry did exert control in the present moment of the play by setting things in motion to end his own life. In light of these considerations, I concluded that Jerry was definitely not the engine operator, but he was some kind of controlling factor within the engine itself.

Central to a combustion engine is the cylinder, a significant working component. As a kind of tube enveloping the piston, the cylinder provides borders and limitations that are essential to allow the engine to run smoothly by trapping the expanding gas, allowing pressure to build, and causing the gas to ignite. This ignition propels the other components of engine forward, making it run. The cylinder represents Jerry, as he is the "central working part" of the entire plot. Jerry arrives at the park looking for the perfect person to help him end his life. Through his dialogue and actions, he sets up boundaries, walls, and limitations, keeping Peter (the only other character within the play) enclosed and trapped.

Through this metaphor analysis, I came to see Peter as the combustible gas, trapped within the cylinder. Under pressure, the gas ignites and causes an explosion. In light of the larger plot of the play, this really made sense to me. At the beginning of the play, Peter and Jerry were strangers, having never met to that point. The audience discovers that Peter has come to the park to mind his own business, escape from family and work, and enjoy a quiet moment with a book. Jerry, however, has other plans. On this particular day, Jerry has come to the park looking for the perfect person to help him carry out his suicidal plan. Jerry needs to find a person he can control, and he finds that in Peter. Once Jerry starts a dialogue with Peter, we can see that that he is creating barriers, prohibiting Peter from escaping. Through his actions and dialogue, Jerry creates obstacles and hurdles, impeding Peter from removing himself from the situation. In doing so, Peter's frustration builds, and because he is trapped within the walls of Jerry's cylinder there is no escape. The combustible gas—that is, Peter's frustration—builds and builds until the end of the play, where it explodes into the final action. Peter, holding the knife in frustration and defense, allows Jerry's motion to lead to his stabbing and death.

Viewing the play, plot, and characters through the metaphoric lens of a machine provided me with a unique way to view the characters, their motivations, and actions. It also provided insights that I believe could have been incorporated into the rehearsal and/or production process. For instance, the idea that Jerry envelops Peter, restraining him into a contained area, could have had implications for the internal and external traits of both actors. I think most actors would naturally conclude that, as a character, Jerry is not in control. His life and situation have been controlled by others for years, and as someone looking to commit suicide he seems to be obviously out of control. But even though his life has been negatively impacted by so many people and in so many ways, this machine metaphor lens allowed me to see that, during the course of the action of the play, Jerry internally feels powerful and controlling. He creates the boundaries for Peter, and in doing so he exerts the majority of the power within the plot. This interpretation would no doubt affect my sense of Jerry's internal state and motives, as well as his vocal and physical traits since power can be shown through volume, inflection, rate, stance, and movement.

In our actual performance, Peter and Jerry almost never came in contact with one another. Considering things through the machine metaphor might have opened up the possibility of more regular contact between the characters. For instance, in order to show a physicalized representation of his control, Jerry (the cylinder) might physically block or restrain the movements of Peter (the gas). Consistent with the synchronized movements of the parts of an engine, Peter might also have found himself taking on the same physical traits as Jerry. For instance, if Jerry made certain movements Peter might have found himself making the same motions, demonstrating how powerful Jerry's control really was.

The director might also have applied some of these insights into the staging process. Because the engine is consistently moving, the director might have incorporated mechanized staging components that reflected that idea constant motion. For instance, since the action of the play takes place in a park, the director could have considered incorporating, for example, a bicycle in the background. Possibly the wheels of the bike could have been in constant rotation, representing the endless movement and repetition of the machine.

Though this reflection back led me to see a number of interesting possibilities, I did actually find it somewhat difficult to apply the machine metaphor. My knowledge of machines (combustion engines in particular) is limited. Because of this, I first had to research and learn about some different machines in order to find the one I believed best fit the action of the play. Although this was a bit tedious for a non-mechanic like me, the identification and understanding of the engine metaphor did lead to real insights that hadn't appeared through my original character analysis. Overall, the structural metaphor of a machine generated insights into relationships, control, power, physicality, and staging that were unique and that I think could have been quite valuable for my character portrayal and for the overall production.

The action of the play as an organism

In order to analyze the script and character using the structural metaphor of organism, I started by asking myself the following kinds of questions. "What is this organism? Are there living subsystems of that organism and, if so, in what subsystem am I living? How can I affect the other parts of the system/subsystems of which I am a part? What specific part of the organism am I? What parts of the organism are the other characters? What does this system need to survive? What is the environment, and what part does it play in all of this?"

Though there are only two characters and the overall form of the play is rather simple, the internal action of the play is rather complex. Therefore, I saw this play as a complex living body, complete with a number of internal subsystems, such as the cardiovascular system, the skeletal system, and the neurological system. Rather than thinking about the body as existing in some larger environment, I decided to conceptualize the entire living body itself as the environment, and the subsystems were elements of the play that interacted with each other as part of that larger organism/environment.

When considering the characters as parts of the body, I found myself thinking of Jerry as the heart and Peter as the brain. I think these understandings initially came from recognizing that, throughout the play, Jerry is highly emotional (heart) while Peter is quite logical (brain). Also, I reasoned that, if the action of the play is a body, stressful moments are essentially times when the whole body is experiencing stress. When the body itself is feeling stressed, the characters as subsystems of the body would have different kinds of biological response. The stress affects Peter who, as the brain, transfers that stress responses to the other areas of the body, including the heart (Jerry). I thought that this perhaps could be understood as the brain sensing stress and then sending a rush of adrenaline through the body which results in a rapid heartbeat and increased blood pressure.

The organism metaphor provided an interesting way to view the relationship between Jerry and Peter. Specifically, it provided some useful insights related to the dynamics of power and control. When we performed the play, I saw Jerry as the driving force behind the plot line. My application of the machine metaphor seemed to suggest that Jerry exerts control over Peter. However, this organism metaphor provides a contrasting viewpoint, suggesting that Jerry might not always be the character in control. As the brain/heart metaphoric entailments suggest, Peter might in some ways be controlling the action of the play—at least until the very end, when Jerry forces Peter to respond with a fight-or-flight reaction. Considering the characters as brain and heart brought up for me questions of the differences between physiological response and psychological response. These are things I never thought about when rehearsing and performing. However, these insights from applying the organism metaphor do make sense when looking deep into the plotline. Jerry comes to the park looking for someone to help him end his life, and he thinks that he finds that in Peter. Throughout the plot, Peter allows Jerry to express his feelings, but Peter interacts in a way that keeps Jerry reasonably in control. Peter does not allow himself to get sucked into Jerry's emotional state and intentions until the very end. For the most part, Peter tolerates Jerry and allows him to have a certain biological response (e.g., high energy, anger, run-on dialogue), but he won't allow him to reach the point of becoming dangerous—that is, becoming a threat to the rest of the body.

Another insight that came from this metaphor analysis related to my sense of Jerry's responsibilities. From an organism point-of-view, Jerry as the heart of the body has the responsibility to regulate the blood that flows to all other subsystems within the environment of the body. If Jerry were to stop working, become too stressed too irritated or manic, he would negatively affect the other subsystems and possibly kill the entire body. Because Peter knows that his survival as part of the body depends on the survival of Jerry, he does what he can to keep him working properly.

Looking at things from this perspective revealed for me some useful insight that helped to clarify for me the relationship between Peter and Jerry. When we were actually working through the rehearsal process, I struggled with the question of why Peter stayed. It didn't make sense to me that Peter would sit on this bench for an hour listening to a perfect stranger ramble on about the negative aspects of his life. But, in viewing Peter and Jerry as interdependent parts of the same living system, a system in which one character's life depends on the other, it started to make sense. If Peter is genuinely concerned about his life and survival, he wouldn't leave, at least not until he felt that Jerry was no longer a threat. If he tried to leave, he might upset the balance of the living organism, throwing Jerry into a "heart attack" that could result in dangerous and deadly consequences—for either or both of them.

These metaphoric insights could have affected choices about both internal and external characteristics for both Jerry and Peter. Jerry might be portrayed as in a state of constant instability, relying on Peter to try to keep him stable. Perhaps the idea of shifting from increased heartbeat to normal heartbeat could have been reflected physically, through the speed of Jerry's actions and maybe even through some kind of tapping or stomping from Jerry in a way that would audibly but subtly suggest a heartbeat. For me, this was a new and unique insight. Until I considered this metaphoric frame for the action of the play, I was not thinking of Jerry as relying on Peter for anything more than his final suicidal act. But the organism metaphor suggests that Peter and Jerry might have a relationship that is far more mutually dependent.

During the actual production, I viewed Peter as simply being standoffish and scared of Jerry. We staged the production to represent this idea. However, it might have been interesting to suggest that Peter is also worried about Jerry—worried that, if Jerry reaches a breaking point, the life of the entire organism (including Peter as the brain of the body) could be threatened. This kind of analysis might have led to less of a focus on Peter trying to get away (which was the focus in our production) and more of a focus on Peter attempting to calm Jerry down through touching, movement, or perhaps soothing vocal techniques.

Through applying this organism metaphor, I can also better understand the final scene of the play. In the final scene, Jerry forces Peter to pick up a knife, on which he then impales himself by running toward it. The biological process of a panic attack provides a way to think about the characters' action and reaction. A panic attack occurs due to a biological malfunction in the brain. The malfunction results in an over-exaggerated sense of threat, leading to increased anxiety. This anxiety forces the cardiovascular system to respond, resulting in an increased heart rate and high blood pressure. The brain believes that it can't control this response, and a fight or flight reaction is initiated.

If a panic attack is part of the action of the play, then, toward the end of the play, a malfunction in the brain must be occurring. It would be interesting for the director and the actors (specifically Peter) to determine where exactly the malfunction transpires because this ultimately sets the climax of the play into motion. One possibility would be to reflect the moment of malfunction through movement. Perhaps there is a moment when Jerry becomes particularly aggressive toward Peter. Perhaps Peter could physically step out of the playing space causing Jerry to fear that he is being left alone. Regardless, in the world of the play, a malfunction in the organism occurs. This malfunction would then trigger a panic attack, during which Peter, the brain of the organism, shifts from rational functioning into strong emotional reaction—fight or flight. Peter picks up the knife. Peter's response could be understood biologically and through the lens of the organism metaphor. During a panic attack, the brain irrationally tries to regain control over all other bodily functions, specifically the heart. In doing so, however, the body spirals more and more out of control. When Peter is threatened, he responds as a brain would during a panic attack, using a rather irrational step to try to regain control over the other systems, escalating the action of the heart (Jerry) and ultimately leading the entire body (action of the play) to a point of crisis.

The main and most important insight arising from this organism metaphor analysis was in my discovery that Peter and Jerry are far more mutually dependent on one another than I ever thought. I had been seeing Peter as someone who essentially sat on the sidelines of life, exerting little control over the people or circumstances surrounding him. A bystander. A character that just had to be there for Jerry's story to unfold. In our production, I felt that the focus, control, and plotline was one-sided, with a concentration on Jerry and his desire to end his life. However, this analysis helped me to understand that Peter has just as much, if not more, responsibility and control throughout the play. While Jerry is concerned with ending his life, Peter is focused prolonging his. Through this metaphor, I came to see that Peter and Jerry are equally important to the progression of the plot, and that their interdependent relationship should be seen as integral to the arc of the play, reflected in a back-and-forth power dynamic.

Even though organisms are generally more complicated things than machines, I found the application of the organism metaphor to be somewhat easier than that of a machine. I think the reason for that is simply because I am more familiar with the idea, components, and functions of the human body—certainly more than I am of a combustion engine. I still had to do some research into the relationship between the brain and the cardiovascular system, but I didn't have to spend much time determining which type of organism was represented the action of the play. To me, the human body is the quintessential example of a living organism, and it just seemed to fit so well to the play.

My almost automatic identification of the human body as the type of organism I wanted to apply did make me wonder about a potential limitation here. I worry that, because it is so immediate and familiar, the body could be too easily and too often looked to when applying the organism metaphor. I would suggest to those considering this approach to character analysis that they might intentionally look for some organism other than the human body as a framework. At the same time, I did find the body metaphor to be very insightful and helpful in exploring the relationship between these two characters. It definitely led to insights that did not arise in the actual rehearsal and production process and that I know would have provided opportunities for further character development, especially in the areas of character motivation and relationship.

The action of the play as a culture

In reflecting back and analyzing the action of the play as a culture, I decided to focus on what I viewed to be the most important aspect of the plot, the suicide. This was the component I struggled with the most during our production; therefore, it was the one that I wanted to explore further through metaphor analysis. As with the other metaphors, I began by posing to myself the kinds questions suggested in the previous chapter. Of those, the prompts that seemed to have the greatest potential related to ritual and symbolism.

It seemed to make sense to think of both characters as engaging in ritual. A ritual is usually understood as a set of actions that are repeated in a specific way and that are recognizable and meaningful to a group of people or culture. In the play, we can see Peter as someone who frequents a certain park and uses the space for a kind of ritualized meditation—almost like a person going to a church or other kind of cultural sacred space for prayer. When Jerry enters what we might call Peter's "sacred space," Peter becomes uneasy and uncomfortable.

These ideas of cultural ritual and sacred spaces could help to explain Peter's strong reaction and response. A sacred space is an important part of a person's culture. Jerry shows a blatant disregard for Peter's sacred space when he enters, interrupts, and forces Peter to literally move from his place of reflection. Jerry's disrespect makes it easier to see how Peter could be moved to violent action at the end of the play. A violent display would not be an abnormal response when people feel that their cultural beliefs, practices, or religious freedoms are being attacked. And if this bench is a sacred space for Peter, then Jerry's invasion is not just a personal inconvenience. It is a challenge to something deeper and bigger and more communal. Defending this space means defending something holy and something that is part of Peter's cultural identify, and it also means defending the space on behalf of all who are part of the larger culture.

Jerry's sacred space seems to be his apartment. He informs Peter about the significance of this space numerous times throughout the play, which demonstrates his recognition of its importance. It also suggests that he knows, from his own experience, that being kept away from a scared space can lead one to violence. In one of the most popular monologues from the play, Jerry describes how his landlady's dog has become an obstacle, keeping him from the sacred space of his room. Because of this, Jerry decides to take drastic action and kill the dog. I now see that there is a strong correlation between Jerry's action of violence toward the dog and Peter's action of violence toward Jerry. Both situations can be considered defense of a culturally meaningful sacred space. During the rehearsal time and production, it never crossed my mind to consider this connection. Looking at these circumstances through the lens of a cultural metaphor, I can see how the two characters' stories are almost parallel.

Jerry's suicide can also be explored through the lens of a cultural metaphor by analyzing it as a kind of ritualistic sacrifice. Human sacrifice has been practiced throughout history in many different cultures. The purpose of sacrifice varies from culture to culture, but an inherent trait seems to be appeasement of some kind, often for a cultural deity, spirits, or the deceased. Ritualistic sacrifice is done to set something right, to atone in some way. So I decided it might be interesting to view Jerry's death as a cultural sacrifice.

Throughout the play, Jerry expresses his desire to be a part of "normal" culture. He has been an outsider for so long, and he has longed to experience life accepted as part of the cultural norm as Peter does: marrying, having a family, living in a large house, having pets, a job, and free time to sit on a bench and reflect on his life and accomplishments. But at this point Jerry has given up. It doesn't seem like he has any hope of being a part of normal culture. Instead, it seems like he now wishes to take action against culture, specifically Peter's culture.

This was for me a very intriguing insight. By following this metaphor where it would lead, I ended up considering the possibility that Jerry was not as interested in ending his own life as he was in ending Peter's. No, not Peter's physical life, but his comfortable normative existence and way of understanding his world. Seeing the action of the play in this way, Peter is actually the one who is sacrificed, and the sacrifice is performed to appease Jerry and his sense of the world's unfairness. Although Peter doesn't actually die, it seems clear that he will not be able to just continue on as he has. After his essentially forced participation in this ritualistic sacrifice, Peter will never be who he was. It is unlikely that Peter will be able to go to his sacred space again. By sacrificing himself, Jerry seems to have recognized that his real place is in the culture of the forgotten, the abused, the disregarded. He was not able to be part of Peter's culture, the culture which he had so desired. Instead, he upholds an ultimate cultural value. Challenging cruel injustice. He does so by threatening the sacred space of someone who epitomizes the unjust culture that made him an outcast.

I believe seeing the action of the play as a culture could have helped us as actors and director. It has allowed me to consider why and how the desecration of one's sacred space could lead to violence. It has helped me to see the parallels between Jerry's violent reaction to his landlady's dog and Peter's violent reaction to Jerry. These kinds of insights did not come out of our actual rehearsal and production process, but, if they had, they would have offered some useful performance possibilities, especially for reflecting intriguing character motivation related to those critical last moments of the play.

Looking back at this production, I can see how the application of structural metaphor has very real potential for assisting in the discovery and presentation of character, in regard to both internal and external character traits. These reflections on my role in *The Zoo Story* show how this approach can be a unique and beneficial character analysis technique. It provided insights for me that had not been revealed through other forms of character analysis. However, this was a retrospective analysis. I did not actually incorporate the approach into the rehearsal and production process. Fortunately, I was able to do so in another production. In the next chapter, we offer my account of that experience.

References

Albee, W. (1998). *The Zoo Story.* Samuel French.

Klaus, C. H., Gilbert, M., & Field Jr., B. S. (2002). *Stages of Drama: Classical to Contemporary Theater* (5th ed.). Bedford/St. Martin's.

7 How this worked for Angeline in *Vanya and Sonia and Masha and Spike*

Note: This chapter is shared in Angeline's first-person voice.

About a year after I performed in *The Zoo Story* (1993), I participated in a production of Christopher Durang's play, *Vanya and Sonia and Masha and Spike* (2013), taking on the role of Sonia. I found Sonia to be one of the most challenging characters I have ever portrayed, and so I was eager to apply structural metaphor character analysis in hope of gaining a clearer understanding of her motivations and desires.

Vanya and Sonia and Masha and Spike is a Tony award winning absurdist play that focuses on the bizarre and irrational relationships between siblings as they come to terms with the death of their parents and their own feelings of insignificance. The following is the plot summary from the Dramatis Play Services, Inc. (2023) website.

> Middle-aged siblings Vanya and Sonia share a home in Bucks County, PA, where they bicker and complain about the circumstances of their lives. Suddenly, their movie-star sister, Masha, swoops in with her new boy toy, Spike. Old resentments flare up, eventually leading to threats to sell the house. Also on the scene are sassy maid Cassandra, who can predict the future, and a lovely young aspiring actress named Nina, whose prettiness somewhat worries the imperious Masha.

As usual for me, I prepared for the role by conducting initial script analysis, exploring the text in order to gain a general understanding

DOI: 10.4324/9781003341024-10

of Sonia's character. Through my script analysis, I examined what Sonia said about herself, what the playwright had written about her in the stage direction, and what others said about her and to her. I also explored her actions and reactions, as they were given in both the text and stage direction. This initial analysis helped me to understand some basic aspects of her character. However, I was struggling to find options for an honest portrayal of Sonia's feelings of worthlessness and depression.

Although comedy is an important aspect of absurdism, the humor arises from an actor's honest portrayal of their character's actions and reactions to the absurd situations surrounding them. Relying only on script analysis, I couldn't find any real honesty with Sonia, and I felt I would end up portraying a caricature instead of a character. I hoped that the structural metaphor analysis process would lead to a better understanding of Sonia's internal traits that could then be incorporated into her characterization through actions, reactions, and vocal/physical mannerisms.

During the early rehearsal process, I started applying the structural metaphors of machine, organism, and culture, and I recorded the process and results of my application in journal form. After we closed this production of *Vanya and Sonia and Masha and Spike,* I took time to review my journal entries. What follows, then, is another reflective analysis examining the effectiveness of this structural metaphor character analysis technique. In contrast to the reflection from the previous chapter, this one is not speculation about what I might have gained from applying the power of structural metaphor but, instead, a report of how structural metaphor actually did contribute to my own character insights and performance.

The action of the play as a machine

In order to analyze the script and character by framing the action of the play as a machine, I asked myself the following kinds of questions throughout the rehearsal process and during my journaling sessions: "If the action of this play is a machine, then what does the machine do? Who runs the machine? What are the most important parts of the machine? What part of the machine am I? What is needed to keep me functioning properly, and do I need any maintenance?"

To examine Sonia's role in the machine, I first had to determine what the overall machine of the play would be. In rehearsals, I noticed that other characters didn't like to be around Sonia, and she seemed to cause and create problems between them. Although the type of machine wasn't initially apparent, I did begin to consider the possibility that Sonia could be characterized as a "virus"—not a biological virus, but a virus for a machine. So I began to think about the action of the play as a computer, and Sonia as a virus within that computer.

Throughout the early journaling and rehearsal process, I tried to incorporate the computer virus metaphor into my characterization; however, as rehearsals progressed, I didn't find this metaphor to be the right fit. I can't think of anything positive or helpful about a computer virus; however, this was not the case with my character. In addition to the problems Sonia brought to the situation, she also was a loving and compassionate person who had spent the majority of her life caring for others. Therefore, I could no longer hold onto the virus metaphor as an all-inclusive representation of her character.

I had worked to apply and extend this machine metaphor analysis very early on in the rehearsal process, and because of this I did expect that there might be the need for some change over time. By the third week of rehearsal, I realized I needed to give up on the idea of seeing Sonia as a computer virus. Even so, I did still have the sense that the overall computer metaphor could be appropriate as a way to frame the action of the play. So I decided to revisit the machine metaphor and work through some of the question prompts again in order to better understand Sonia's role in the machine and the relationships and power dynamic between her and her siblings. This time, my analysis led me to consider the possibility that Masha could be understood as the computer operator, Vanya as the computer processor, and Sonia as a file within the computer. Because I still did view Sonia as having some "viral" qualities, I ended up thinking about her, not as a virus, but as a computer file that occasionally becomes infected by a virus.

These extensions of the computer metaphor really helped expose for me some aspects of power and control within the sibling dynamic. As the machine operator, Masha makes all of the decisions. She decides when the computer will be on, when the computer will be off, and what programs need to run. She demonstrates this power within the play by controlling the action and the characters through the provision of monetary resources. Masha pays for the house, the food, the bills, the help, etc. Vanya and Sonia have never had jobs and do not contribute to their living situation in any way. If Masha weren't there as the operator, the machine (computer) would not run.

Early on in the rehearsal process, it became apparent that Sonia had a lot of resentment toward Masha. Although Sonia's lines offered some justification for this resentment (e.g., "I took care of your parents." "You just left us here."), I struggled with the amount of resentment Sonia harbored toward Masha, and I wanted to explore contributing factors other than Masha's rejection of her parental responsibilities. The machine metaphor helped lead to insights relating to that resentment. I considered that, because Sonia recognizes that Masha holds the role of the machine operator, she accepts that her life and actions are in fact controlled by Masha. If Masha doesn't open the Sonia file, then Sonia can never be an active component within the machine. Sonia's role in the machine/computer/action of the play is completely dependent on Masha. Recognition of this dependence results in resentment toward Masha and leads to feelings of extreme anger and sadness.

I felt I was able to effectively incorporate these insights into Sonia's characterization. I knew that Sonia resented Masha for not helping out with her dying parents, but I also knew that the resentment ran much deeper than that. Using the machine metaphor helped me to realize that Sonia resents Masha because she possesses the power. As a file, Sonia believes that Masha controls her life, and without Masha's permission she can never be opened and will never experience connection and a sense of being useful and valuable.

While Masha seems to exert the majority of the power and control within the action of the play, Vanya also seems to wield some power over Sonia. Because of this, I viewed Vanya as the central processor (CPU) within the machine. Although the operator still has the majority of the control, Vanya can pass down commands to other parts of the computer. Throughout rehearsals, I started to see that Vanya often tried to pass commands down to Sonia by offering advice. Additionally, when Sonia's virus would surface—typically as boredom, pain, regret, resentment, and jealousy—Vanya would try to combat the virus by making jokes or by comforting her in times of stress. By doing so, Vanya was perhaps performing a virus check or initiating some virus software as a kind of maintenance on the Sonia file. All of this was surely something that had been commanded by Masha (the operator) during one or more of her visits.

At the start of Act I, Sonia is not functioning well as a file. It occurred to me through this metaphor analysis and the rehearsal process that, in order for the Sonia file to run properly, she had to be "opened" from an outside source. At the end of Act I, the operator (Masha) opens the file (Sonia) by inviting her to a party, and this provides Sonia with the opportunity to open and run properly and at her fullest capacity. But, as my metaphor analysis suggested, the virus is always there, lurking somewhere deep within the file. I experienced this insight during rehearsal and performance, specifically when Sonia receives a call from a young gentleman expressing interest in meeting her for dinner. I imagined this new situation as one where the Sonia file has been copied to a different computer run by this new operator (the young gentleman). Although Sonia is excited at the opportunity of engaging with and responding to a new operator, she still experiences the virus in terms of self-deprecation, sadness, and fear. Even at the end of the play, while Sonia has begun to feel a slight amount of hope, the viral symptoms of sadness, resentment, and regret are lingering just below the surface. Like a computer virus, Sonia's feelings are difficult to shed. Although the symptoms may come and go, and though Sonia might have opportunity to be copied to a different computer, the virus will most likely always be a part of the Sonia file.

Though it may seem like an odd way to think about this character and the action of this play, viewing things through the metaphoric lens of a machine led to many insights that I was able to incorporate into the rehearsal and production process. Specifically, this metaphor helped me to further examine aspects of power and control within the relationships of the siblings. As I stated earlier, I knew that Sonia harbored resentment toward Masha because of Masha's abandonment. However, the metaphor analysis helped me to consider that Sonia felt resentment toward Masha also, and maybe primarily, because she perceived her as the controlling force of her life. These insights led me to explore various emotional and physical responses to Masha that I was able to incorporate into my characterization through thought processes, motivations, actions, reactions, and physicality. My intent was to constantly reflect Sonia's recognition, fear, and resentment of Masha's control.

Overall, I found framing the action of the play as a machine to be very beneficial, and I truly believe that it provided unique insights that would have not been discovered through other forms of character analysis.

The action of the play as an organism

As with the machine metaphor, my application and exploration of the organism metaphor occurred fairly early on in the rehearsal process. Within the first few rehearsals and without really even realizing it, I was already starting to view the action of the play as a body, with a focus on interdependent subsystems that rely on and affect one another. This made obvious sense to me because the action of the play deals with complex family dynamics among three siblings and how they have affected each other in the past and present. Though in the last chapter I cautioned against too quickly adopting "the body" as the specific framework choice when applying the living organism structural metaphor, it really made so much sense intuitively for me in this case. So I embraced it.

Throughout my journaling and the rehearsal process, I posed the same kinds of question prompts that guided my retroactive analysis from the previous chapter: "What is this organism? Are there living subsystems of that organism and, if so, in what subsystem am I living? How can I affect the other parts of the system/subsystems of which I am a part? What specific part of the organism am I? What parts of the organism are the other characters? What does this system need to survive? What is the environment, and what part does it play in all of this?"

Similar to what occurred from my application of the machine metaphor, my perception of Sonia and her role within the organism changed throughout the rehearsal process. Early on, I concluded through experiences in rehearsals that Sonia was fragile and delicate and should have fragile and delicate characteristics. She seemed highly emotional and seemed very dependent on the strength of others, specifically Vanya. I started to play with the idea that Sonia was part of the skeletal system because, to my thinking, bones seem rather fragile because they can break. However, the more I explored this metaphor, the more I fought against it. There certainly are delicate parts of the skeletal system—for example, a finger, a toe, or a clavicle. However, it dawned on me that, overall, the skeletal system actually exudes strength. While Sonia had demonstrated moments of strength throughout her life (taking care of her ailing parents), I could not see strength as one of her core qualities. Also, the skeletal system is responsible for protecting and carrying all of the internal organs and internal systems. While Sonia could be seen as offering a kind of protection to her parents, overall, the protection of others does not seem to be one of her responsibilities. Therefore, the skeletal metaphor didn't seem to be the right fit, and I began to explore other options.

It didn't take long before I started thinking about how Sonia's emotional instability could be perceived as a sickness, and usually this sickness was brought on by the people or circumstances surrounding her.

Before continuing on with how I explored and extended this organism metaphor, I need to note something. I recognize now how this idea of sickness in a body is quite similar to the idea of a virus in a computer. I am guessing you may also see this similarity. But at the time I was applying these metaphors and initially journaling about them, the two ideas seemed completely independent to me. Also, I think it is interesting how my initial direction with the idea of Sonia being the skeletal system just didn't work, and so I went in a different direction. This was quite similar to the path I followed when applying the machine metaphor. Thinking back, I am sure these ideas and the ways the two metaphoric frames evolved were related, one prompting the other or maybe both influencing each other. Maybe this interplay between these ideas and these interpretive frames only goes to show the richness of structural metaphor and the ways that exploring multiple metaphors can be beneficial. I think this is something worth noting, and so I wanted to point it out here. But to avoid getting too sidetracked, let's get back to my consideration of Sonia's emotional instability as a sickness.

As I played with this idea of sickness, I also considered whether Sonia should be thought of as the "heart" of the body because of her strong emotional qualities. However, because the heart doesn't as far as I know often succumb to common illness, I ended up not pursuing that metaphor extension. I was still drawn by the fact that Sonia seemed so deeply affected by those around her, and, at the same time, she also possessed the ability to deeply affect others. I spent some time just reading general information about interdependence in the human body. I stumbled onto some discussion of the importance of the human immune system, and for some reason it resonated with me. I learned a bit more about how the immune systems acts as the body's defense mechanism, recognizing the healthy cells of the body and trying to eradicate anything that is unfamiliar.

I found this way of extending the metaphor to be a perfect fit! Sonia seemed to reject anything that is unfamiliar and alien. This realization led to some amazing insights that I directly incorporated into Sonia's characterization and my use of the playing space. For example, I decided I was going to find a way to, metaphorically, create a healthy immune system environment by incorporating "healthy cells." These are the cells that establish and maintain a robust immune system. In the production, they took the form of various props and costume pieces: a fancy writing pen, a book of word finds, a robe, brightly colored socks and slippers, a crown, etc. I started incorporating these props and costumes into the rehearsal process. I found that these healthy cells assisted in keeping my character (i.e., the immune system) focused and emotionally healthy. I also found that if Sonia didn't have these healthy cells, the immune system became weak. Sonia would exhibit this weakness through irrational emotional responses and behaviors. For instance, when Sonia returns from the party, she is visibly agitated. In order to reinstate her healthy immune system, she immediately surrounds herself with healthy cells (putting on her socks and slippers, working on her words search). Conversely, when Masha steals Sonia's crown (another healthy cell) during an argument, Sonia becomes weak and spirals into emotional turmoil.

Once I had solidified Sonia's role within the subsystems of the body metaphor, I shifted my focus to the other characters. Masha's power and control led me to initially view her as the brain of the body. However, because her presence and actions so directly seemed to affect the immune system, I didn't find this metaphoric extension to be appropriate. Instead, I began to view Masha as a virus (this time a biological rather than technological one), first causing Sonia to withdraw into sickness, and then causing Sonia to fight for her life. As soon as Sonia gets word that Masha is coming for a visit, the immune system is being attacked. Sonia starts to become weak, and this weakness was displayed through symptoms of unease, anxiousness, and fear. I started to incorporate some of these ideas directly into my physicalization of Sonia by rubbing my neck and shoulders, wringing my hands, shaking my knees, and scratching and pulling at skin.

I also used this metaphoric extension to better understand Sonya's erratic responses to Vanya. Because the immune system is weak, it becomes easier for Sonia to succumb to illness (actions and dialogue that she finds upsetting) and react irrationally. For instance, when Sonia discovers that Vanya has poured himself a cup of coffee, she responds irrationally by hurling the cup onto the floor. Perceiving Sonia as a weakened immune system helped me to understand and motivate her response. When an immune system is weak, it doesn't have the ability to fight off illness. Similarly, Sonia doesn't have the ability to fight of strong emotion and respond in a rational way due to the stress that Masha's visit has placed upon her.

The concept of cellular barriers also came to mind when thinking about the relationship between Sonia and Masha. The immune system has the responsibility of creating biological barriers to keep viruses and bacteria at bay. Similarly, as the immune system in the action of the play, Sonia might attempt to create barriers between Masha (the virus) and herself. Much of the play had already been blocked prior to this realization; therefore, I wasn't able to really incorporate these into the staging or my characterization. However, I did try to demonstrate the existence of barriers through subtle body movement and facial expression. For instance, I found myself often turning my body to face away from Masha when speaking, and I also made facial expressions that indicated Sonia was intentionally not recognizing, and therefore obstructing, Masha's emotional appeals.

Vanya is a stable, unwavering character, who provides strength and emotional support for the other characters. For me, there is a natural connection between the idea of emotion and the heart, so I considered looking at Vanya as the heart of the body. However, Vanya is more than just emotional support for Sonia; he is a fundamental source of health and strength. As such, I decided to consider Vanya as a vitamin, building up the immune system and helping it (Sonia) to fight off illness. This insight built on what I had come to understand about the relationship between Sonia and Vanya, and it allowed for a real understanding of interdependency to develop. Throughout rehearsals, I found myself thinking about the organism metaphor and discovering ways that Sonia needed Vanya in order to ward off the illness cause by Masha. I demonstrated this through suggesting a closeness with Vanya that was vastly different than the closeness Sonia felt with any other character. For instance, in the performance, Sonia never touched or was touched by anyone other than Vanya. When Sonia needed strength, she would "take her vitamin" by sharing a glance with Vanya, standing close to Vanya, or touching Vanya.

Viewing the play, plot, and characters through the metaphoric lens of an organism led to many insights that I was able to incorporate into the rehearsal and production process. Specifically, this metaphor helped me to further examine aspects of sibling relationships and personal characterization. Understanding Sonia as an immune system helped me to recognize why she acts and reacts so negatively toward Masha and relies so heavily on Vanya. Through the use of the metaphor, I was also able to create an environment based on the metaphoric entailments of healthy cells, leading to certain props and costumes that became an integral part of Sonia's characterization. In fact, on the second night of production, I couldn't find Sonia's pen. Because the pen had become such a significant part of the metaphor, I found real difficulty in using another pen, and I know this negatively affected my performance and focus. As was true with applying the machine metaphor, I found applying the organism metaphor to be very beneficial, providing unique insights that would have not been discovered through other forms of character analysis.

The action of the play as a culture

In exploring the action of the play as a culture, I began by posing to myself the kinds questions suggested earlier. As was true with my retrospective application of this metaphor with my role in *The Zoo Story*, ritual as an element of cultural became an important consideration. This is because of some very interesting connections I made between the ideas of culture, ritual, repetition, anxiety, and food. Let me explain.

Early on in the rehearsal process, I found myself struggling to both manage and expose Sonia's battle with anxiety. I had played similar characters in the past, and I was now finding myself falling back on past characterizations instead of finding new and unique ways to portray Sonia. I am someone who has personally struggled with anxiety, and I know from experience that one way to deal with it is through repetition. My anxiety often lowers if I go through a series of actions in a prescribed order. Given my personal experience with managing anxiety and the challenge I was feeling in portraying Sonia's anxiety, the idea of ritual just jumped out at me as I was considering various prompts related to the culture metaphor. Ritual virtually always involves some aspects of repetitious action. We were already some weeks into the rehearsal process, and I had not yet in any intentional way been playing with the idea of repetition as part of my performance. But when this connection between anxiety, repetition, and ritual dawned on me, I was quite eager to see where the culture metaphor might take me.

Ultimately, ritual as reflected in repetitious action became a key factor in Sonia's characterization. This particular way of exploring the culture metaphor especially helped to explain and justify some of Sonia's seemingly irrational actions. For example, within the first three pages of the play, the dialogue escalates into an early dramatic climax when Sonia shatters a coffee mug by hurling it onto the floor. I struggled as an actor to find the motivation behind the action, especially since there didn't seem to be enough time or dialogue to create an appropriate and realistic build. Viewing the action through the lens of a cultural metaphor allowed me to frame Sonia's act as a response to the interruption of ritual. Sonia finds pleasure and comfort in the ritualistic repetition and routine of bringing Vanya coffee, and when she enters the morning room and finds that Vanya has poured himself a cup of coffee, her ritual is interrupted.

Recall from my retrospective analysis of *The Zoo Story* that, there too, I discovered how interrupting someone's ritual can result in violence. When Jerry's ritual was interrupted, he tried to kill his landlady's dog, and when Peter's park bench ritual was interrupted, he defended himself with a knife. Similarly, when Sonia's ritual of bringing Vanya coffee becomes interrupted, she reacts violently by breaking the cup. By viewing this scene through the metaphoric lens of cultural ritual, I could much more easily understand Sonia's drastic action, and I found myself able to portray that action in a more motivated and believable way. The metaphor helped me to see the coffee ritual as something sacred to Sonia, and any disruption to that ritual would understandably have devastating effects on her already fragile mindset.

Within the action of the play, I also began to realize that food might be understood as a valuable cultural commodity. I recognized early that there were a good number of lines and scenes focused on food (e.g., "I brought you donuts." "I paid for everything, even the food." "Couldn't you make us a light lunch?" "Lunch is served!"). Because of this, I also recognized early on that food could be incorporated into Sonia's characterization through "stage business." As a performer, I often incorporate stage business such as cross-stitching, sewing, reading, working a puzzle, etc. For some reason, stage business for me often includes eating or drinking, and all the food references in this script made this an easy choice. However, through my exploration of the culture metaphor, and because I knew that Sonia was a very anxious character and was searching for ways to alleviate her stress, I decided to consider my incorporation of food as not simply stage business but part of an important cultural ritual. I could fairly easily incorporate eating food in a way that was consistent with the script, the repetition of this behavior could be motivated as a way for Sonia to deal with her anxiety, and the idea of this being part of a cultural ritual could allow for some useful metaphoric extension to enrich the performance.

One way I extended this idea of food as ritual was by recognizing that, within certain cultures, food also symbolizes closeness, togetherness, and membership. Although Sonia's parents are deceased within the world of the play, I decided to create a backstory where food was an important aspect of their family culture. It was quite natural for me to explore this because I have had a lot of personal experience with food as part of family culture. I come from a large Italian Catholic family, and I understand the importance, symbolism, and cultural significance of food. In my family, it doesn't matter if you are visiting for the weekend, attending a wedding or funeral, or just having a Sunday dinner, large amounts of food and drink are imperative. Food is also used as an important aspect of ritual in commemorating loved ones who have passed on. For instance, in my family we make certain traditional foods like gnocchi, cioppino, pizzelle, Easter bread, and Hungarian cookies in order to summon and renew a connection with our deceased loved ones. These kinds of food rituals can be an important part of a family's culture, and I wanted Sonia to have a connection with her parents that could be experienced, understood, and represented through food.

In rehearsals, I started to think of the kinds of foods that Sonia would have access to. As she doesn't often leave the house and doesn't ever speak of cooking, I decided that Sonia could indulge in the ritual of junk food, specifically the kinds of junk food she would have had access to as a child. These foods would be easy for the housekeeper to pick up and would require little preparation or cooking time. I started incorporating cheese puffs, cookies, crackers, Cheese Whiz, Coke, and donuts into the rehearsal process in order to play on the idea of food rituals. In terms of character motivation, I understood Sonia as using the food rituals to establish comfort, security, and the kind of predictable redundancy that can help manage anxiety. The food rituals reminded Sonia of her childhood that fostered a connection between her and her deceased parents, something that would bring her comfort. Food became a very important aspect of Sonia's characterization, and, eventually, food was incorporated into every scene.

Viewing the action of the play through the metaphoric lens of a culture led to many insights that I was able to incorporate into the rehearsal process and into my performance. By understanding Sonia's desire to participate in daily rituals, I was able to empathize with and meaningfully portray her intense anxiety and seemingly irrational behavior. Through the use of this metaphor, I was also able to see so much of the action of the play as based in cultural ritual. I discovered motivating stage business and developed my character more fully and cohesively. As with the metaphors of machine and organism, I found the structural metaphor of culture to be truly valuable. It provided new and unique insights that I do not believe would have been revealed through other techniques I have used.

So, in wrapping up this chapter and this book and as a final word of encouragement from both of us, we invite you to seriously consider the power of structural metaphor. We hope you found our introduction to Lakoff and Johnson (1980) and their ideas about metaphor as central to human thought intriguing. We hope you see as we do the real possibility of applying structural metaphor as a strategy for rich character analysis. Though these two last chapters focused on showing how an individual actor can apply this approach for character development, we hope you can also see how this could be embraced and applied more collectively by a whole cast or company, serving both as a tool for character analysis and as a unifying framework for an entire production.

As we indicated earlier, the possibilities are limited only by the imaginations of those who decide to give it a try. When you do give it a try, please remember to have fun, because playing with metaphor is fun. Serious fun. Follow where the metaphors lead, and expect good things. We are confident that doing so will lead you to the kind of deep and profound character analysis that results in stronger and more compelling performance.

References

Albee, W. (1998). *The Zoo Story.* Samuel French.

Dramatis Play Service, Inc. (2023, September 4). *Vanya and Sonia and Masha and Spike: Christopher Durang.* www.dramatists.com/cgi-bin/db/single.asp?key=4655

Durang, C. (2013). *Vanya and Sonia and Masha and Spike.* Samuel French.

Lakoff, G., & Johnson, M. (1980). *Metaphors We Live By.* University of Chicago Press.

Index

For Product Safety Concerns and Information please contact our EU representative GPSR@taylorandfrancis.com
Taylor & Francis Verlag GmbH, Kaufingerstraße 24, 80331 München, Germany

www.ingramcontent.com/pod-product-compliance
Lightning Source LLC
LaVergne TN
LVHW010938110826
845149LV00013B/2659
* 9 7 8 1 0 3 2 3 7 6 0 6 6 *